The Khaki Road of Yesterday

Dedication

This book is in deepest appreciation for all the men and women that were involved in WW1. My son Gus C. Zimmerman and his wife LaWanda C. Zimmerman are instrumental in getting this book publish with the invaluable help and support of Debbie Gioquindo.

This book was published from the original manuscript written in 1940.

The Khaki Road of Yesterday

Copyright © 2017 by Gus and LaWanda Zimmerman

First edition

All rights reserved. No part of this book may be reproduced in any form, whether by electronic or mechanical means, without written permission from the author's family: Gus and LaWanda Zimmerman and publisher, Gus Zimmerman. It is permissible to use a brief quote in the body of a critique or review article discussing the book.

The scanning, uploading and distribution of this book via the Internet or via any other means without the permission of the publisher is illegal and punishable by law.

All brand names, product names, and company names in this book are trademarks or trade names of their respective owners. The author and publisher are not affiliated with any product or company mentioned in the book unless otherwise stated.

Cover design by Emanuel and Ernest Cole "The Fotoshoppe" Cary NC

Photos from Family Album

Interior Layout by Gus and LaWanda Zimmerman

Edited and Transcribed by Debbie Gioquindo

ISBN: 978-0-9981540-2-2

E-Book ISBN: 978-0-9981540-3-9

Published by Million Dollar Sips LLC

THE KHAKI ROAD OF YESTERDAY

AN AUTOBIOGRAPHY WRITTEN BY

JOHN B. KANE

FROM ENLISTMENT TO DISCHARGE OF WWI

GIVEN TO HIS YOUNG DAUGHTER AT AGE 10

Foreword

I'm amazed this brilliant yet so humble man was my father. How the horrors of a war can change a free spirit of a 24 year old draftsman who volunteered in WWI in the army to fight for his country. This happen to my father. His memory of the Great War was never spoken, only by writing of this book. I'm now 87 years old, and my dad has long been gone, but beautiful memories remain with me. I hope you will enjoy reading this book with some funny, dramatic moments. A masterpiece!

His daughter,
Sashie

TABLE OF CONTENTS

Sashie Age 10, 1940

The Khaki Road of Yesterday

Letter to Sashie

Sashie, you are going on eleven years of age. I know what I am writing will not be fully understood by you just now, but some time later, when you grow a little older, I think it may be of some good to you.

What this little preamble embodies will be of little value to anyone, only to you and yours to come after. I would like you to pass it on as the years roll by. Some day perhaps you will have children and they will in turn have children and it may, in a personal sort of way, give you and them a little story of the times as they were during the days of the World War of 1914-1918.

True, those days have long since passed and are recorded in the history of Time, but as generations move on they will, I believe, become more significant.

The world moves in great cycles and reflects the philosophy and culture of its existence in the movements of these transition periods. Just as the arts stamp the history of man through these changes: the caves to the Stone Age, lake houses to Early Primitive, pyramids to the Egyptians, the Acropolis to the Greeks, the Colosseum to the Romans, the Gothic Catedrals and the Renaissance to the continental Europe of the middle centuries, Georgian to the Victorians, and the modern to the machine age.

All these periods record a distinct change in the thoughts and actions of men destined to become leaders of their times. Through their dynamic force they moulded the cast of their

followers and led them along the path to peace or
through the treacherous byways to war.

The pages of history reveal the milestones
along the world's path have been marked by bitter
conflict, and it seems much easier to find the
records of tyrants who wielded the power of
destruction through the ages than the defenders
who fought courageously to preserve the peace of
their people.

The days of which I write were, I believe,
the beginning of a new cycle, the dawn of a new
and perhaps a wicked philosophy, created from the
great upheaval of tormented and bewildered souls.
New leaders rode in upon the wreckage of 1918 to
again recast the shattered molds according to
their own wicked designs, and history continues to
type the unfinished pages of the great struggle of
1914-1918. What the pages will reveal when this
great cycle closes, no one knows; but I am sure
the happenings that made possible this little
story I am about to relate were the birth of the
new social order.

It is not my intention to try to impress
upon you the great deeds or the heroism of any one
individual or group, but rather to weave this
little story around the lives and experiences of
millions of men of whom I was a small part, so if
you see the letter "I" repeated quite often as I
ramble on, keep in mind it is just an echo of what
thousands experienced. My life as a soldier varied
little from that of my comrades. We had moments
when the air was full of laughter and song, when
youth held sway and would not be downed, and we
had other moments when the heart-strings pulled
tight about our chests and it was hard to bring a
smile to the surface of our sun-bronzed cheeks.

This great adventure we call life is very
fantastic. The great stage is ever before us and
it seems the footlights never dim. The drama goes
on and on, like the earth revolving around the
sun. We all have a part, - some are destined to
play the leading roles, while others make up the

great cast, - but no matter what we do, great or
small, each helps to piece together the great
pattern of the drama of our times. And so it is
with this in mind that I want to leave with you a
few pages of recollections, showing as they unfold
a segment of the stage, together with the lives
and reactions of the characters who made up the
cast that fate had destined to play a part in the
great struggle across the sea.

1914 - 1916

At the outbreak of the war I was working as a draftsman in the office of an old established firm of Architects. In the early spring of 1914 a friend of mine working at the board next to mine approached me on the idea of a trip to Europe. He advised me he could make arrangements to travel over on a cattle boat. We were young and had a very little money, and that was a cheap way to get passage. In return for your trip, your duties consisted of playing chamber-maid to the animals.

A lot of the boys went that way and I thought it was a swell idea. It would give me a chance to see the works of the old masters. I could make sketches, take photographs and in a general way get a well-rounded bit of education that I felt would help me a lot in the coming years.

I was very enthusiastic about the trip and spoke to Nanna about it. She objected very much to the whole idea, and the result was that my friend sailed without his chamber-maid mate. It was to me a great disappointment, as I bade him goodbye one bright sunny day in late spring. But Nanna was right, as mothers usually are; because a month or so after he landed war was declared in Europe and it was some six or seven months before he returned. He told me later that I was very lucky, that his trip consisted mostly of finding some way to get passage back to this good old country.

After war was declared, conditions in this country became uncertain and confused, the stock market had violent fluctuations and closed for a time, business in general took a sharp slump. I

was laid off and drifted from one office to
another for some time.

It was not long, however, before the wheels
of industry were humming again. War orders began
pouring into this country from Europe. Plant
expansion started to increase, and the ovens of
the big steel mills were blazing with molten metal
taking the shape of shells. I secured a position
in the drafting room of one of our large chemical
plants. They were just embarking on a tremendous
expansion program. Buildings grew like mushrooms.
I was busy and very happy and somewhat conceited,
I guess, walking around the plant with a bunch of
blueprints under my arm, giving instructions to
the various contractors.

I don't believe I had ever earned over
fifteen dollars a week before I secured this
position; now, in 1916, at 23, I was making
thirty-five to forty dollars a week, holding a job
with a little responsibility and gaining in
experience all the time.

1917

In the spring of 1917, on April sixth, our country declared war against Germany. As far as I can remember, it was of little concern to me. I did know that for some time past we had had a considerable amount of trouble with Germany in relation to our position on the seas. The great British liner Lisitania had been sunk with the loss of a number of American lives, and ships sailing under our flag had been attacked and sent to the bottom, but I was busy, young and carefree. I did not realize the seriousness of the situation.

At any rate, we were at war with Germany. The machinery was put in motion for the registration of men eligible for service and I, together with millions of other young men, was called upon to register for my services when called.

The summer of 1917 was a glorious one for me. A friend working at the plant invited me to spend the months of July and August in a little vine-covered bungalow along the banks of the Rancocas Creek in New Jersey. He and several friends rented the place every year and spent the summers there. It was a delightful spot, situated about a mile and a half up the creek from the Delaware River. Big oaks and maples spread an abundance of shade on the low pitched roof, and honeysuckle vine covered the wood trellis at the sides of the gravel walk that led to the float along the stream.

We commuted every day by train, and twenty minutes after we left the plant we were at the Torresdale pier along the Delaware. Old Jim, who always maintained a faithful schedule, ferried us across the river in his one lung skiff and up the

winding stream. Martha, our colored cook, always
watched for us, and as we turned the bend she
would wave her bright colored apron in salute and
scamper her 180 pounds up the hill and into the
house, where the chops or steaks would be waiting
to take their plunge into the hot buttered pan on
the blazing wood stove.

What a time we had! And what a set-out
every evening! Big juicy cuts soaked with butter,
and fresh vegetables of all kinds from old Jerry,
the farmer who lived along the sloping bank just
above us. Jerry and his faithful pal, Laddie, a
big collie, lived alone, and many a time in the
the stillness of the night we would hear the soft
notes from his harmonica floating downstream as he
sat on the porch under the glow of his swinging
lantern, with Laddie at his feet.

The early evenings were spent in diving in
from the float and splashing around in the cool
smooth waters of the stream, and then a paddle
upstream or out to the broad waters of the
Delaware, where speeding motorboats cut through
the gentle swells and trim boats with white sails
bellying in the evening breeze, gliding gracefully
by.

On moonlight nights we sat on the float and
watched for the lights on the little tug that
towed the sand barges many miles upstream to the
sand pits at Hainesport. As it turned the bend we
boarded our canoe and waited for our friend Sam.
He was a good old fellow and loved to tell his
little jokes. He always perched on the end barge
with his legs dangling over the rear end, and his
corncob pipe seemed to throw as much smoke as the
little tug ahead.

After our usual greeting, "Hi Ho, Sam!" the
tow rope was thrown, and we settled against our
back-rests to enjoy the beauties of the night.
Bill played his ukelele, everything seemed so
quiet and peaceful, just the chug of the tug and
the swish of water along the sides of the barge;
now and then the hoot of an owl carried across the

silent stream, as if to greet a passing traveler.
The creek wound in graceful curves and great trees
lined the bank. Heavy branches arched the span and
met in midstream, where the moon blinked thorough
the rustling leaves, like a mass of twinkling
stars.

The minutes passed all to swiftly on these
trips, and it was always with a heavy sigh that we
gave Sam the signal to cast off, and turned our
course downstream again.

I will never forget that summer. I had no
thought of war, nor of the misery surrounding our
times. To me it was a world of sunshine and
happiness, of peace and contentment. The beautiful
open country with winding streams had been my
playground. There could be no wrong amid such
surroundings.

There is something wholesome and
invigorating about youth, and as I grow older I
sometimes feel the world would be a lot better off
if the spirit and the thoughts of youth could
prevail, instead of the cunning and sinister
thinking that sometimes comes to man with
maturity.

The stages of development in humans are
quite mystifying. We have a period of openness, we
live for the joy it offers. We are lighthearted,
full of laughter, taking the hurdles with an easy
stride. Then as we grow older, some of us develop
an air of independence; we become more serious;
selfishness begins to sprout. We watch more
closely the march of our friends, what they are
doing, and how they do it; the power they possess
and the worldly materials they accumulate: and
sooner or later, whether we realize it or not, we
are right in step with that hard, ruthless grind
on to what is known as Success and Power.

Those words are all ablaze at the top of
the ladder. Some reach there, but many fuss and
fume and stumble, and fight each other all the way
along the path, and so it is with nations. Nation
is pitted against nation in all the bloody horrors

of war, as men climb over the broken and torn
bodies of other men, like the beasts of the
jungle, in their maddening rush to reach this
mythical goal.

I would like to see you, Sashie, live your
life in a simple way. Do not mar your life or lose
the good things it offers, by racing all the time
to reach the top rung. Who knows the inner
thoughts of those who arrive and survey their
holdings from the summit? To some I know the view
is cold and barren and they are dreadfully
lonesome.

It may be you can do more to enjoy the
fulness of your life by mingling with the crowds
and helping those who have stumbled on the way up.
Do not misunderstand me. I want you to go forward,
I want you to keep in line with your time, but I
would hate to see you trample over your friends
and neighbors to inherit a synthetic success.
Also, try to keep selfishness, jealousy and greed
for power out of your heart. This treacherous trio
has run rampant through the ages: they led the
slaughter in ancient times, they carried me across
the sea to take part in their war of blood and
hate: and today they are sweeping across land, sea
and sky, spreading again the wreckage of souls
that leads to a land of darkness and desolation.

I see I am drifting. I have no desire to
bring into these few pages any semblance of a
sermon, but I suppose, as this story unfolds,
there will creep in now and then a disorganized
rabble of words.

The Realities of War

The summer was over. The leaves began to
turn to the brilliant hues of approaching Fall.
The crisp winds of September nights swept through
the air and it made one feel quite comfortable to
sit before the logs at the open fireplace and
enjoy the relaxation of delving into the pages of
a favorite story.

War was far from my mind, but fate works in
strange ways. One afternoon in late September, a
buddy of mine to whom I had become quite attached
stopped at my board and told me he was thinking of
joining the Army. He was leaving shortly to see
Major Charles A. Pierce, an Episcopal mimister who
lived on Girard Avenue, a Senior Chaplain who had
spent many years in the service. He was called to
Washington by the Commanding General and
authorized to form an organization in the U. S.
Army, to be known as the Graves Registration
Services. It was an entirely new department in the
service and was to be patterned after the
organization then in operation with the French and
British Armies in France.

I listened intently as my friend outlined
the duties of the service more in detail. I was
warming up, and at the end of the conversation
decided I would go down with him to see the Major,
and we made arrangements to see him the following
day.

That evening I spoke to your Uncle Jim
about the whole affair. He was only nineteen, and
not in the draft age, but he became very
enthusiastic and decided to go with us. I didn't
want him to jump too fast and cautioned him about
the seriousness of the move. I had practically
made up my mind to enlist and I could see that his

reaction was about the same. I told him, however, to sleep over it, and if he felt the same in the morning he could go along.

The following afternoon the three of us met the Major, and kindly gentleman, somewhere in his sixties. He explained to us that he wanted good, clean-cut men in the organization, and that we would see active service, and at times would be subjected to the dangers of the Front Line troops. He talked to us for a long time, going over every detail in the most careful manner. He also advised us that the first unit then being formed was scheduled to leave for France in three weeks. He finally left it in our hands to make the ultimate decision.

After the conference we went into a huddle outside his office, and fired with enthusiasm, decided to enlist. We returned and advised him of our decision. He clasped our hands and wished us luck. We left immediately for the recruiting station.

Fort Slocum

It was not long before the preliminary examinations were over and in a day or so we found ourselves on a train bound for Fort Slocum, New York. We met some thirty or forty boys on the train. Conversation was brisk, all wondering what was the great adventure before us would bring.

We landed at New Rochelle, a short distance from the Fort, about nine o'clock in the evening. It was one of those raw September nights and a slight drizzling rain was falling. Going through the waiting room, at the station a jolly looking fellow, dressed in a light suit with a big flower in his buttonhole, hailed us. "If you boys are going to Slocum, jump in the bus outside." We later found he was one of the leading citizens of the town, spending all his time at the station greeting the boys and furnishing transportation. That was his way of doing his bit. I do not believe he ever realized the good he did. It was not so much the ride that counted, but the friendly and unexpected greeting in a strange town, just when you needed it most.

I will never forget that first night at Fort Slocum. Those were the bluest hours of all my army experience. I would have given anything in the world just to be in my old bed at home once more. We were met at the gate by the sergeant in charge. He herded us into a little room and examined our luggage. I have laughed many a time over my outfit. Nanna sent us on our way as if we were going on a summer vacation: socks, underwear, pajamas, sport trousers, silk shirts, and neckties galore. The sergeant took one look at my outfit and wanted to know where my golf sticks and slippers were. "Whadda you guys think this is, a

hotel or watering place? Just because it's along
the water, don't think it's a Coney Island.
Afterwhile I guess I'll find some of you guys got
a bathing suite tucked away somewhere."

The Sergeant's remarks may sound funny now,
but it was far from funny that night. A good sized
lump came into my throat and my right arm felt as
if it wanted to go straight to that soldier's jaw.
With all the vehemence I could command, I said,
"My mother packed that suit case." He saw I was
disturbed, and his old army heart softened
somewhat. He grabbed me by the arm. "O.K., Buddy,
I know. My mother's just the same. Ain't they all
the same, but hell, what a job they give me at
this inspection post!"

Well, after the general inspection was
over, the sergeant delivered a well rounded
lecture, while we stood holding our suitcases like
a bunch of lost orphans. In substance, it was
this. We had all arrived loaded down with too much
junk; that we would have no further use for
clothes; we were in the army now, so we could
either send the load home, or a clothing agent
would be in the camp the following day and we
could sell him our remains, suitcases and all.

I must confess my first half-hour under the
wing of the army was not very encouraging. It
seemed to me a hard, cold conception of life. Why
should anyone enlist to give his services, yes, to
offer his life for his country, and be treated in
such a way?

I could not help but feel, as we left this
first encounter and trudged our way up the dismal
walk to the barracks, that life was all wrong.

We arrived at the barracks under the
guidance of another Sergeant, were assigned to our
bunk, ordered to take a shower and go to bed. It
was with a heavy heart that I slumped into my
first army bunk. Sleep, for me, was not around.
Soon I could hear soft noises, sounds brought on
by memories that crept into hearts, not the hearts
of weak men, or men afraid, but just such as you

might hear when kittens or puppies are away from
their mothers for the first time.

I was deep in thought when I heard the rap
of a stick on one of the uprights of a bunk. It
was from the sergeant in charge of our barracks.
In a loud, bellowing voice, he advised the
assembly that the real men wanted to sleep. If the
sobbing sisters continued to have a monopoly on
the air he would move them to a barracks of their
own.

What time I drifted off to sleep I do not
remember, but I do know this - - no night after
that, whether it was under the stars in the wide
open spaces, in the barns, or under the shelling
of enemy fire, did I fall asleep with the pangs of
heart-ache as I did that night.

The first morning at Fort Slocum dawned
bright and clear. The bugles sounded through the
cold crisp air at 6:15. We hustled into our
"civvies" and marched to the large mess hall at
7:00, for our first army meal. Another surprise
was in store for me. I had always been accustomed
to frizzled beef for breakfast: you know I still
enjoy it. What do you suppose we had? Beef stew. I
lost my appetite right away. A big husky fellow
across the table, who had evidently gone thought
his initiation a few weeks before, yelled, "Hey,
soldier, shove the battleship this way," and down
it came, a big china bowl that looked something
like our cut glass punch bowl. He took three or
four helpings and piled it on his plate until it
looked like an Egyptian pyramid. I didn't eat much
breakfast that morning, but it was not long before
I was digging into my meals the same as my friend
across the table.

Our first day in camp was a busy one. When
we enlisted in Philadelphia we had a preliminary
examination. Now we were subjected to a very rigid
physical examination. It lasted until about four
o'clock in the afternoon. Your Uncle Jim and I
passed. The friend we enlisted with, and who was
responsible for our enlistment, failed and was

sent home. He was a good boy, physically fit, but
it seems he had broken his arm as a youngster and
could not touch his shoulder with the tips of his
fingers. So you see how rigid the examination was.
Now it was time to receive our uniforms and
equipment. We all lined up and walked along a long
counter. About every five feet a soldier looked us
over; each handed out a piece of wearing apparel
or equipment. Upon reaching the end of the counter
we had everything from shoes-laces to mess-kit.
After we received our equipment, we asked where we
could change into our uniforms. One soldier
standing in the doorway yelled, "hell, there ain't
no women around here! Start right in." So we sat
along the curb of the drive and the magic of
changing a civilian into a soldier was performed.
They made a pretty good-looking soldier out of me,
but some of the boys looked as if they had been
shot at and missed.

Well, I was in the army now, and I felt
very proud in my new uniform as I marched up the
path to the Y.M.C.A that evening to write my first
letter home to Nanna.

Fort Slocum
Sept. 21, 1917

Dear Mother:

Here's a few lines to let you
know we arrived safe last evening. We had a very
pleasant trip over, the only thing, we arrived in
a raw drizzling rain and it was quite late.

When we landed at the Fort
they took our life's history, which lasted about
one-half hour, then examined our luggage and
razzed us for carting so much stuff along: these
old army fellows are tough customers but I guess
that's what it takes to make a good soldier.

After all the preliminaries
were over a big husky sergeant gave the command to
fall in line and we all marched up the road to the

barracks. We were ordered to take a shower and then proceeded to a big room loaded with wooden bunks.

The Sergeant stood in the center of the room, told us to get undressed and flop. "Snap to it, lights out in ten minutes." He put me in mind of an impatient father getting his bunch of kids to bed.

We were up bright and early this morning and have been going through a rigid physical examination all day. Jim and I passed this afternoon and we are now wearing our uniforms. We met a couple of nice fellows who are connected with our unit and have spent most of our free time with them. It makes you feel much better when you have good fellows to chum with.

They have a swell Y.M.C.A here and that is where I am writing from.

Sitting around me are a couple of hundred fellows writing letters. I think this will be all tonight, as I am very tired - - off to the bunk for me.

Be good to yourselves.
Your son, John
P.S. Don't worry a bit, we are o.k. and everything is going along fine.

The next morning we lined up for our first reveille. The top sergeant in charge of us was a husky regular army boy, and as Irish as they come. With our equipment we received two pairs of shoes. One pair was a light tan, the other dark tan. I put on the light pair. We were standing at attention, with the sergeant eyeing us over. He happened to look at my shoes. "Who told you to wear them shoes?" in a voice to make you quiver. I told him I received two pairs and just decided to put this pair on. He informed me the pair I had on was my dress shoes, that I should have worn the darker pair, known as duty shoes. I replied, "Well, I am just new here, how the hell should I

know that?" He never said a word but gave me a
look that indicated all was not well in Uncle
Sam's army.

It wasn't long before I found out. After
mess I heard his commanding voice again, "Private,
report to Sergeant Smith at the Mess Hall." My
buddies at lunch time had the pleasure of seeing
me wheeling big drums of coffee on a truck, all
through the building. I kept that job for three
days straight. It was a tough assignment, but it
did me good. I was not quite so cocky after that.

I think my stay at Fort Slocum lasted about
eight or nine days. As yet we had not been
assigned to our regular outfit. It gave me a
chance to mingle with the boys from all over the
country and already I was getting a good
education.

Fort Jay

From Fort Slocum I was sent to Fort Jay on Governor's Island, across from the big city of New York. Here I was assigned to my regular outfit. Our Captain, fresh from civil life, hailed from Washington. Lieutenant McCormick, an infantry officer, a member of the Second City Troop of Philadelphia, and who had seen service on the Mexican border, was second in command. He was a fine soldier, every inch of him; a youngster not more than twenty-four. He had plenty of pep and plenty of guts. A fine disciplinarian, and never asked for too much, never expected you to go anywhere or do anything that he himself would not measure up to. As this little story moves along, I am sure his name will pop up from time to time.

Life at Fort Jay brought new experiences into my life. Gradually the mold was being cast. I was losing the identity of my former self. Civilian clothes, silk shirts, socks, neckties, cuff links, stick pins, handkerchief tucked neatly in the top pocket of my coat, all seemed so far away. A bugle sounding taps in the clear silent air of night telling you the day is finished, crawling in under your blankets amid the grey canvas of your home, awakening with the sharp shrill notes of reveille rolling over the coming dawn seemed the order of the day. Here at Fort Jay I received my first real soldiering: Guard duty, Manual of Arms, policing, squad formations, and parading.

There were some amusing incidents that occurred in my stay here.

I was assigned to guard duty one morning from 2 to 4 A.M., along the water front. Of course we had received no fire arms at this time. As I

remember, they gave us a club, something like the
club you see policemen carrying. I was dutifully
guarding my section on the front. Presently I saw
someone in uniform approaching. He passed and we
bid the time of morning. A few paces beyond me he
stopped and returned. "May I inquire your business
here at this time of the morning?" I told him I
was on guard duty. He asked if I knew my duties as
guardian of the waterfront. I assured him I did
and that was to challenge anyone who might come
along; if they did not halt I was to blow my
whistle and spread the alarm. "Very well," he
said, "what about me?" I passed and received no
challenge. "Well, you're in uniform," I replied
with an air of confidence. For fifteen long
minutes I received what you would call a good
bawling-out from the officer of the day. In the
wee hours of the morning I was receiving a good
education on one important phase of Uncle Sam's
Army. His final admonition was that enemy spies
sometimes do dress as American soldiers. We
rookies did some funny things. Joe Sherman, a
Jewish boy whose folks lived in Brooklyn, was
coming across the parade grounds one night from
leave. The soldier on guard challenged him. He
kept right on going. Finally the final challenge
came, "Halt, or I'll shoot." It was good that he
did halt, the soldier on guard was an old-timer
and happened to have a rifle loaded with real
lead. Joe told us all about it when he arrived in
the tent. His reasoning was, as he explained to
the guard, "Why should you stop me, can't you see
I'm a soldier in this man's army the same as you,
and furthermore, I'm just as good as you." "Fine
qualities for a good soldier, but rather dangerous
if you keep it up," was the guard's reply to Joe.
      I think the most embarrassing thing that
happened was the time all the rookie companies
paraded in front of the Commandant of the fort.
      For a week previous we had been on the
parade ground, drilling for the important event.

Finally the great day arrived. Our captain
insisted on giving the commands.

As we arrived in front of the reviewing
stand, the Captain wanted to show us off. He gave
the command "Right oblique." That's where the fun
started and where we separated. Half the company
turned to the right, and for some unknown reason
the other half turned to the left, and there we
were, approaching the enemy from all angles. The
command came to halt, and halt we did. We looked
like a bunch of strayed sheep. The Captain was in
a real stew. He didn't know the command to get us
into position again. Finally, in desperation, he
came over to my side, which happened to be the
lost battalion, and said, "For God's sake, side-
step as gracefully as you can over in back of the
rest of the company." I don't know how gracefully
we got there, but nevertheless we became as one
and the parade went merrily on.

Fort Jay was a very interesting place to
me. During my spare hours I paced every bit of
ground. Castle William, the prison, was
particularly interesting. Its appearance reminded
me of an old medieval relic with its sombre stone
tower and cold stone walls.

One day I happened to meet a guard of the
prison at the Y.M.C.A. I expressed interest in the
prison and asked if there was any chance of going
through. He arranged a trip for me and it was well
worth while. It did me good. I resolved then and
there that I would do nothing during my army life
that would get me within the walls of a prison.

A few days later, while walking down the
path leading from the officers' quarters, I
noticed a trusty raking leaves. No one was around.
I stopped and offered him a cigarette, which he
accepted gladly. He had gray hair and was slightly
stooped; to judge his age was rather difficult,
his face appeared youthful, yet his movements and
the deep-set lines around the mouth indicated many
years of life.

This had been my first opportunity to talk
with a prisoner. Many times in Fort Slocum and
here I had watched them marching along under
guard. There seemed always an air of mystery
attached to them: to see but never to know.

He leaned on the rake and took a couple of
deep inhalations from the cigarette. A faint smile
broke around the deep set mouth. "Well, soldier,
how's things going?" I told him I was just a
rookie, had only been in the army about three
weeks, and wasn't quite sure yet how things were
moving.

For want of something better to say, I
suppose, I informed him of my visit to the prison.
He told me that was home to him, even the island
comprising Fort Jay he had come to love. "You
know," he said, dropping the rake and seating
himself on the leaves in the barrow, "I have been
on this island a long time. The skyline over
yonder has changed much and the dazzling lights
against the black of night have increased until it
looks like a fairyland. It must be a great city by
now. I can well remember how it was when they
ferried me across here years ago, but today it
must be changed a lot. They tell me the
automobiles are crowding the streets and the
horses don't seem to be afraid of them anymore."

As he talked and reminisced a peculiar
feeling came over me. It struck me hard. I felt
as if he was miles away from all I knew. Just an
echo from the distant past.

I said to him, "It must be pretty tough
going for you." He just smiled, put his hand on my
shoulder, and said, "Don't worry about me, buddy.
I am content. The outside world don't mean much to
me anymore. I have paid my dues in this world long
ago. I'm on pension now. I went against Uncle Sam
once and he made me pay the price, but he is just.
He never let me go to bed hungry, nor did he ever
let me sleep cold at night, and he never kept me
away from my God. The blow that stings and never
lets up," he continued, "is, he deprives me of the

honor of wearing the uniform I love. He dresses me
in the blue denim of a prisoner, but that is his
business, and more than that, it is a warning to
you, young soldier. Be careful as long as you wear
that outfit. Remember always to carry yourself
with honor and dignity; never forget the great
responsibility that uniform carries. Some day you
may be alone amid the screeches of shells and all
the damnable noises of hell. You may, within your
own heart, be scared, you may be covered with
filth and mud as you crawl along in what they call
No-Man's-Land, but never falter, never turn back
and above all never let that uniform down. Better
it be with all its mud that it covers your cold
and lifeless body in a shell hole on the field of
battle than to have it replaced by the blue denim
that stands before you now. "

Well, Sashie, I kind of fussed and fumed
around a bit. I tried hard to keep the tears away.
Why not? - after all, I was a soldier. Nanna was
proud of me. She told me so in her letters: what
a brave boy I was, going to war - the most cruel
and bloodiest war the world had known; and yet the
tears did come. There was nothing much I could say
to what looked like an old man standing before me,
only this - - I grabbed his hand and said, "If I
remain half the man in uniform that you are in
blue denim, God knows I'll be satisfied."

We never met again. That evening we had
instructions that reveille would be sounded at
4:30 A.M. The following morning, under cover of
early dawn, we were ferried down the river to
Hoboken, to begin our journey for the great
adventure across the sea.

I will never forget that man. By this time
the prisoner of Castle William can be no more. God
has pardoned him, and I know he is wearing the
uniform he loved, - I can see medals of valor
pinned upon his chest. Not that he fought in any
great battles on the fields of France, but because
he fought a great battle within himself - a battle
that knew no retreat - a bitter conflict that

surged within his soul every night as he lay on
the crude bunk allotted to him in Castle William.
        I do not desire to eulogize a prisoner,
Sashie, nor do I want to impress upon you that bad
men should not be punished for what they do
against society. What I do want to leave you with
is this - - do not judge persons too harshly.
Remember, all persons who walk the streets and
enjoy the freedom of the laws are not good people,
and all people behind prison bars are not bad
people. Human nature is odd at times; we can not
tell how things are going to turn out. So do not
be to critical in your appraisal of people who
have slipped from the crown of the road, just
remember we all have a long way to travel along
this ever-changing path.

Hoboken

When we arrived at Hoboken the sun was just breaking through the bulky cluster of clouds in the east. The heavy frost of October put a mantle of silver upon the camouflaged steel hulls of liners swinging lazily at their morings. We were told our outfit was to sail on the George Washington. It was a massive looking thing. Already thousands of troops were strolling on the decks. Everybody seemed to be happy, - - one group of soldiers yelling greetings to the others; some singing "Where do we go from here, boys?" In general, it looked more like the start of a trip down the river on a one-day excursion boat.

Somehow or other we mixed signals and found ourselves marching up the gangplank to a shop-worn freighter. Before the war it plied between New York and the southern ports, and was owned by the United Fruit Lines. It carried the name Tenadores. Later it went to a well deserved rest at the bottom of the sea. On a return trip to America it was torpedoed off the coast of England. We looked our new home over with somewhat of a disappointment. There was no holiday spirit on board the Tenadores.

We were assigned to our quarters in the forehold of the vessel. Wooden bunks had been built, three tiers high, with a piece of canvas nailed to the uprights. Passageways were about 2' - 6" wide. There were no ventilation except through the opening in the deck hatch. An old wooden ship ladder led from the deck. The only light was from a few electric bulbs scattered here and there.

About three o'clock that afternoon we noticed a contingent of colored boys come to a

halt along the gang plank. They numbered about
three hundred. They were not in regulation uniform
but wore an assortment of everything. Some had
blue breeches and civilian coats, some had blue
coats and civilian trousers, while others wore
blue denim overalls. Footwear ranged from high top
boots to canvas sneaks. All wore vivid blue
overcoats with flashy brass buttons and capes
attached. The capes were turned over their
shoulders displaying the most brilliant colors of
yellow and red. Some had regulation campaign hats,
others had civilian caps, while some had no
headgear at all.

It was the strangest looking conglomeration
I ever saw. They seemed to be in a daze; they gave
sickly smiles to us lined along the rail and I
suppose we returned sickly smiles to them. We were
all wondering if by any chance they were to be our
fellow-passengers on the way over. Pretty soon a
shrill order came from the officer in command and
like a flock of sheep they walked slowly up the
gang plank. They were led over to the hatch and
down the steps to share their allotted 3' x 6'
with us.

Some time later I went down to look my
belongings over, and found one fellow stretched
out on his bunk, quite at home. He was directly
across the passage from me. A good, clean-cut
looking boy and a typical Southerner. He told me
they had been traveling all night, arriving from
the south just a few hours before.

I inquired why the strange outfits, who
they were and what place they held in Uncle Sam's
army. "Hell, Boss, we ain't in the army. We're
stevedores, they're going to use us to unload
ships." He told me they had had a lot of trouble
keeping the boys together, but after the white
boss had shown them the overcoats the stevedores
were to wear, they all wanted to join up. He
jumped from his bunk, put on his coat, and posed
at full length for my admiration: just as proud of
his outfit as you will be when you wear your first

evening gown. I found later that the uniforms were part of an old collection from the Spanish American War era.

We now had on board two colored for every white man. Our Major began to get a little concerned about discipline. He wasn't sure of the reaction at sea in case of storm or emergency. At this time we were not armed. So there was a hurried consultation among the officers, and a company of infantry from the Rainbow Division, fully armed, was assigned to our ship.

Ours was not a troop transport, it was primarily a freighter loaded with a war cargo, and its troop capacity was very small in comparison to some of the other liners.

Toward evening, some of our southern friends became restless and a fight broke out that looked serious for a time. Knives came out of hiding and the infantry boys were used to good advantage. Orders for fixed bayonets were issued, guard posts were established and the deck took on the appearance of strict military discipline. The men were searched and all knives and razors were confiscated.

John Kane "Grand dad", John Kane,
Mary Kane "Nanna", James "Jim" Kane
Mary Kane, Paul Kane, William "Billy" Kane,
Charles Kane.
Saul St. Frankford, Northeast Philadelphia.

This picture was taken October 1917 prior to
leaving for France

Off to France

Around 7 o'clock the cargo hatches were closed, the booms were strapped down, the ship's activities increased, the crew hustled back and forth; ropes were hauled in, a slight shudder through the vessel and we were silently sneaking away under the cover of darkness.

I stood leaning against the rail, the bright lights of New York sparkled in the water, whistles tooted and ship bells clanged as little tugs and ferries made their way through a maze of river traffic. Everything about us seemed so restless and noisy, yet on board there was a strange silence.

As I was standing alone, deep within my own thoughts, a big burly colored boy tapped me on the shoulder. "Boss, are we on our way to New York now?" "Brother," I said, pointing across the river, "do you see those bright lights over there? Well, take a good look, that is New York. It will be some time before you see it again." I never saw anyone so dejected. He told me the white men in charge of their outfit had promised them two days in New York to have a good time before they sailed for France. I told him I felt sorry for him, that I did not believe this was a local, and that we were headed now for the open sea. He left me hurriedly and shuffled down the deck to spread the news to his mates.

The last thing I remember gazing at was the big Colgate electric clock: it was 7:45. I had had enough and called it a day. I walked down the wooden steps into the dimly lighted hold and jumped into my bunk. The motion of the boat as it ploughed toward the great open spaces soon put me to sleep.

Life on the seas opened a new avenue of
experience for me. We zigzagged across the ocean
for thirteen days. The second day out we picked up
other transports and were accompanied by four
destroyers and a large battleship. We learned
afterward it was the biggest convoy that had left
America since the declaration of war. Our convoy
was made up of miscellaneous outfits like
ourselves, hospital units, intelligence service,
signal corps, and a major portion of the 42nd
Rainbow Division.

We all had various duties assigned to us on
board ship. I was assigned as waker-up. My job
was to scamper around the bunks and on deck and
get the fellows up for guard duty. I was on from 2
to 4 A.M. and you can guess it wasn't an easy job
to get some of the fellows on their feet. Many a
time I would get the wrong fellow awake, and the
greeting I received was not a happy one.

The colored boys gave us no trouble at all.
In fact it was a Godsend they were on board. They
were full of life and many an hour was passed
watching them jig and shoot craps, also listening
to sweet melodies of Southern airs as only the
colored people know how to render.

To watch a crap game was a revelation.
Usually 15 or 20 would form in groups, and what a
game! They had no money, only the few pennies we
would throw to them as they danced a jig or sang a
song.

Everything imaginable was in the center of
the ring at these games; collar buttons, cuff
links, shoe-laces, safety razors, shaving cream,
combs, socks. I saw one fellow down to his last
possession rip off a couple of brass buttons from
his uniform. Another fellow threw in his Bible,
saying he hoped the Good Lawd and his mammy would
forgive him. They would do anything, give anything
just to stay in the game.

I will never forget one night. We were
eight or nine days out, and were in the danger
zone. Everyone was more or less conscious of

submarines, and all were under orders to wear life
preservers or carry them with us at all times.
This night, three or four big games were on in the
hold. I was down there at the time. Suddenly a
colored boy came down the steps and hurried over
to his bunk. He grabbed his life preserver and ran
up the steps again. Sooner than it take to tell, a
mad scramble was on, dice dropped, and the booty
was forgotten. The colored boys ran to their
bunks, grabbed their life preservers and made for
the hatch. A jam immediately occurred at the steps
and no one could move. You never saw such a mix-
up. Fists flew, legs kicked in all directions, and
everybody pulling and yanking at each other and no
one getting anywhere. Someone on deck heard the
commotion. After yelling down a few assuring
words, quiet was finally restored. It seems this
colored boy reported for duty. The sergeant
noticed he did not have his life preserver, and
immediately started to give him a good bawling
out, ordering him to go to his bunk as soon as
possible and get his life preserver. The boy
obeyed orders a little to realistically and that
was the reason for the panic. I have often
wondered what would have happened to us in the
hold that night if a real emergency had existed.

     Fortunately there were four or five days as
we zigzagged through the Gulf Stream when the hold
was occupied very little. Everyone took their
blankets and slept on deck; the air was very balmy
and gently breezes swept across the deck like
midsummer.

     I was never so hungry in all my life as I
was on this trip. Rather a fussy eater and just
coming from civil life, try as I would I could not
relish the food on board. In the first place, it
was all steam cooked, and the musty smell of the
Mess Hall that resembled our sleeping quarters was
too much for me. A majority of the boys never used
it at all, preferring to sit around on deck and
eat their meals. One day was quite amusing. We
were going through the Bay of Biscay. We hit an

exceptionally rough sea. The boat pitched and
rolled like a cork. You could hardly hold your
balance, with the result that potatoes, carrots
and chunks of meat left the mess kits and rolled
crazily across the deck. All the colored boys
that weren't seasick had good appetites, and
anything that came rolling their way was promptly
seized. It was a field day for some, while others
were out of luck.

One day I got so hungry I asked a member of
the crew if it was possible for him to get me a
little fruit. I said "The way I feel, fifty cents
would be nothing, if only I could get my jaws in
the middle of a nice juicy orange." If the bribe
meant anything he never showed it. He just
shrugged his shoulders and marched off down the
deck. I can remember as plain as if it happened
yesterday. If I only had the power, if I was only
in the position, of that boy at the time, what a
wonderful world it would be!

I ambled off down the deck and picked a
quiet spot on one of the life rafts at the stern
of the ship. The sea was calm, the sun was bright,
the lazy breezes of the Gulf Stream swept across
the decks. I watched the wake of the sea as our
ship crept along. Seaweed floated about, twisted
and curled as if to resent the presence of anyone
to disturb its peaceful slumber.

My mind was traveling fast as I looked upon
the vast expanse of water. I wondered if some of
it, just a little perhaps, has ever traveled up
the Rancocas Creak I loved so much. Why, the sea
looked so calm I could grab a paddle and set forth
with my canoe and travel upon the silent waters. I
could picture our old colored cook in her colored
apron, serving me fried sirloin with luscious
gravy, steaming corn piled high on the plate, big
fresh tomatoes floating in a mist of cracked ice
with a touch of vinegar and sliced onions. It all
seemed like a dream. I have no desire to picture
my condition so black, but I was somewhat like the

traveler on the desert who sees the mirage of a
watering hole.

I sat there watching the sun sink lower
toward the western horizon. Suddenly I was
brought back to life. "Where have you been all
afternoon? I've traveled the decks high and low
for you." I looked up. It was my friend I had met
at noon. He reached into his blouse and brought
forth a big yellow orange. "Here, take this," and
planted the orange in my hand. Before I could say
a word, he said, "Now stay put, soldier, I'll be
back." A few minutes later he returned. "Well, is
your first course over?" he asked, as he passed me
a little package done up in a nice white napkin
with the ship's name done in blue. It had a
warmth as I took it in my hands. I opened it with
eager eyes and what do you suppose? --two hot
rolls with slices of bacon! I will never live long
enough, no matter what happens, to ever again
enjoy a bacon sandwich as I did on that day.

When I finished and licked my chops, I
reached into my pocket and pulled out a dollar
bill. "Buddy, I'm going to raise the ante a
hundred percent. Here, take it!" He just pushed
my hand aside. "Listen, it was worth five bucks of
my money just to watch you dig in, -- you enjoyed
them, hey, what?" The best I could get him to do
was to take a cigarette. We sat there talking for
a couple of minutes and off he went.

Walking along the deck the next morning I
met him again. He pulled me aside and told me the
menu that day for the gobs was pretty good, steak,
home fried potatoes, peas and coleslaw. "Now
listen," he said as he pulled at the buttons on my
blouse, "I'll get you on ship duty and that'll
entitle you to eat at the crew's mess. Report in
the main salon at ten thirty and I'll fix you up."
Promptly at ten thirty I was there. My job was to
swab up the floor of the main salon. I don't
remember whether it was a marble or linoleum
floor. At any rate, I soon found myself on hands

and knees with a big bucket of soapy water and a
rag, going over the floor.

So far on the trip I had never had any
semblance of seasickness. A lot of the fellows
started the first day out; some of them were in
such bad shape it was impossible to delegate any
of the ship's duties to them at all. In a sense
maybe they were fortunate -- I don't know which is
worse, seasickness or the pangs of hunger.

I wasn't on the job long before I began to
get a queer feeling in my stomach. The longer I
scrubbed, the worse I felt. Finally I had to give
it up and come on deck for air. I tried it again,
with the same feeling. I suppose the rolling of
the boat and my head bent over looking at the
floor did the trick; at any rate, the second time
on deck everything came up and that was the end of
my housework. My good Samaritan caught up with me
around noon time. I explained to him my
unsuccessful attempt at earning my meal. He
laughed and said, "That's all right, you did your
best. Stay on deck and get some good fresh air in
your lungs, and come down to the crew's mess hall
at one thirty and I'll see that you are taken care
of." I appeared after the regular mess was over,
and did I enjoy that meal!

Strange as it may seem, I never met him
again, but I will never forget him. He was of the
many I met during this great walk through life
whose memories the age of time can not dim. Two
days later we passed Belles Island off the coast
of France and steamed into the quiet waters of
Loire to St. Nazaire.

John sits in front,
brother Jim to his left.
Picture taken somewhere in
France.

St. Nazaire

St. Nazaire was a charming sea coast town.
We arrived in darkness. Faint flickers of light,
twinkling like stars, guided us along the shore,
as we silently felt our way to the quay. Shrill
orders, the throwing of ropes, and the last
shudder of the great steel hull as the engines
stopped, told us our sea journey was at an end. We
were in France, the France we had read so much
about, the blood pit of civilization. Where men
were battling against each other. Where cannons
and instruments of sea and air were dealing in
death and horror on a scale never known during the
history of mankind. It was all hard to believe, as
our ship and we settled alongside the deserted
dock, waiting for the coming of dawn.

I rolled and tossed quite a little that
night, wondering what lay before me. What would
we see tomorrow? What did a French city look like?
How did the French people live? What sort of
people were they? It must have been a dream, for
the dawn was upon me. Already I was walking the
deck and the sun was peeping above the horizon. It
was a beautiful morning, not a cloud in the sky.
Everything seemed so quiet. Soon little men clad
in grey were standing on the cobblestone street,
gazing at us. Life was starting another day. Men
were busily engaged in the waters of the quay
lifting sails on small fishing smacks, preparing
to go to the fishing banks for their daily haul of
fish. A sausage balloon was rising in the sky to
begin its day's work of guarding the harbor. The
tile roofs of the town were losing the dampness of
the heavy dew of the night, as the sun rose higher
in the heavens; smoke floated lazily in the air
from the chimney tops as the logs in the open

hearths curled flames around the blackened pots
swinging from the iron cranes. It was breakfast
time in France; the dawn of a new life for me.

Across the quay stood the unfinished hull
of the great liner "Paris." In better days,
hundreds of men had labored on this future giant
of the sea. It was to have been the pride of the
nation. There it stood, alone and deserted since
the declaration of war, like a ghost of the ages.

Big booms swung out over the ship, dropping
large crates of war cargo to the street. A tiny
engine that looked like a toy compared to our big
engines was puffing and snorting, pushing a few
tiny freight cars around. Little fat men in aprons
were pulling trucks with iron wheels clattering
over the cobblestones. Everybody seemed so busy,
each attending to his own little job. Army trucks
with stevedores arrived and started the job of
assorting the newly arrived cargo. Planes were
flying overhead and a big dirigible nosed its way
in from the sea.

Noontime found us standing at attention on
the cobblestone street, awaiting marching orders
to the camp, which was situated on the outskirts
of St. Nazaire, some three miles away. I was quite
excited and felt mighty important as we swung
through the town. "Bon Americain!" "Bon Soldat!"
Little American flags held tightly by small tots,
kisses blown by charming girls, a tip of the
chapeau by the elderly men as the standards went
by, shop-keepers standing in the doorways, waving
their aprons they had taken off for the occasion.
It all seemed so real and personal, not the
boisterous, noisy demonstration of holiday spirit,
but a deep and sincere welcome. Somehow or other
it gave me the feeling I had been away a long time
and was now marching home to the ones I knew. The
strange distant feeling I had had a few hours
previous as I watched the rising sun casting rays
on the roofs of the homes covered with the early
morning mist, was no more. I was one of them now.
The spirit stayed with me for twenty- xxx months.

I traveled far and wide, saw the big cities, and
the tiniest of hamlets. I broke bread with the
well-to-do in houses surrounded with all the
elegance of Louis XIV. I also sat on an old wooden
bench in front of a great stone fireplace stained
with the age of many years, watching the dinner
cook in the old iron pot above the flaming fire,
held by the old rusty crane. It was the meal of
the peasant, plain, but what a wealth of welcome
was tucked within its offering!

Yes, everywhere in France the hearts and
homes of everyone were opened. Even the stars in
the heavens seemed to glisten like twinkling
diamonds as you dropped in the open fields to call
it a day. Little did I think, as our giant liner
steamed away from Brest in late July 1919, that
France, twenty-one years later, would again be the
land of desolation and misery, conquered, in the
hands of her former enemies. What has happened to
the France I knew? Surely that great spirit of
love, courage and devotion to country cannot be
gone. It must rise again. The soldier of France
is not dead, nor will the peasant of France
surrender his plow. Leaders will come from the
true soil of Verdun; they will be the defenders,
the fighters, not the betrayers and cowards of
France.

All the way to camp, youngsters trailed
along with us. We could not understand their talk,
so we just made signs and exchanged laughs. The
camp was well situated on a great level piece of
ground surrounded by beautiful countryside.
Barracks were stretched for miles, it seemed, with
a big parade ground in the center. We were
assigned a barrack and our company became as one
family for the first time. Until this time, we had
bunched with other troops. It didn't take long to
get adjusted to our new surroundings. At the head
of the company street we established our kitchen
and mess quarters.

Our own cook, Tony, a Portuguese, got into
action for the first time. We were very much

concerned over Tony. No one knew anything about
his professional talents. They were as mysterious
as his personality. Tony was about forty, six feet
tall, slightly stooped, and trudged along with the
biggest set of feet I ever saw on any person. He
spoke with a strong foreign accent, and somehow he
seemed out of place in an American uniform. Of
course he was a naturalized citizen and had been
in the country some fifteen years before we
declared war.

After mess, Tony was the most popular man
in the company. He came through the test with
flying colors. Roast beef, mashed potatoes with
good brown gravy, peas, creamed cabbage, pickles
and hot biscuits that just melted in your mouth,
was his first offering. What a change from our
meals on the boat! I gained steadily in weight, my
skin took on a deep tan from the outdoor life,
muscles developed and hardened. I never felt
better physically. No one can criticize Uncle
Sam's treatment of his boys. We always had plenty
to eat and of good quality, and abundance of
clothes and blankets to keep us warm. Of course
there were times when we longed for a good hot
meal, and times when we were cold and covered with
mud, but war is a heartless game and that was to
be expected. A day or so after our arrival I sent
my first letter home.

> *Somewhere in France*
> *November 2, 1917*

Dear Parents:
> *I suppose you will be glad to hear
from me once more. It seems like ages since I
wrote you of our departure while on the boat at
Hoboken. Jim and I arrived at our port safe and
sound.*
> *I had a slight case of seasickness
for a short spell but outside of that everything
went along O.K. Our camp life here is very good.*

*The country is really beautiful. As you stroll
along the open roads one would imagine traveling
in good old Pennsylvania.*

*No doubt you worried a little during
the last few weeks, but cheer up now and let your
troubles slide away. I would like to tell you of
some of our experiences on the sea but we can't
say to much now as our letters must pass the
censor.*

*The type of architecture here is
vastly different from home. Most of the buildings
are of stone or stucco covered, with small
casement windows, decorated with gaily colored
curtains and abundance of flower pots rest on the
wide window sills. The roofs are of tile, aged to
a dull brownish red. The people appear to be very
kind. It is funny to see the little kids with
their quaint costumes rattling along the
cobblestone streets in their wooden shoes.*

*Well, dear folks, I must cut this
letter short. I will try and tell you more as I
become better acquainted on this side of the of
the water.*

> *I am*
> *Your son*
> *John.*

We started intense training -- drilling on
the parade ground, long endurance hikes with full
pack, and plenty of exercise with the shovel as we
worked on further camp expansion. We were among
the first 75,000 troops in France. When we
arrived, there were three American Divisions. The
First arrived in June, the Second in August and
the Twenty-sixth in September. Our convoy that
arrived November 1st, carried a large part of the
42nd Rainbow Division. In December, the 41st
Division arrived. So you see there was plenty of
work to do getting things in shape for the many
thousands of troops yet to come.

I was in the first squad to get leave from
camp to visit the town of St. Nazaire. We had a

great time looking things over. All the shops
appeared to be well stocked. The pastry shops
looked especially inviting, with cakes of all
kinds and shapes. Little French girls dressed in
black, with neat lace embroidered aprons, were in
back of the counters, and we felt quite flattered
as we stopped to window-shop to see them run to
the windows or come to the door to greet us. We
talked and they talked, but neither side made much
headway, they shrugging their shoulders and we
just grinning a bashful adieu.

Finally we landed in a cafe, as soldiers
sometimes do. I had one cognac, and then a strange
craving for peanut candy. I started out to look
for a confectionery store, and whom should I meet
coming out the door but Major Pierce. I saluted
and told him of my desire. He gave me a queer
look, scratched his head and smiled. "Well, I can
speak a little French, suppose we see what can be
done." We tried in several shops, but all he got
was a shrug of the shoulders and "<u>Non</u>, <u>non</u>,
<u>Messieurs</u>." Finally he told me I had better get
back to my squad, as it was getting late.

We left the big clock that stood in the
square in the center of town at nine o'clock, and
started back to camp. And thus ended my first
visit to a French town.

I paid many a visit to this quaint town of
St. Nazaire before we left camp. I got to know
some of the shop keepers very well. I bought many
little souvenirs to send home, and was especially
fond of the little handkerchiefs with American
sayings and designs embroidered in the colors of
our flag. Nanna has many of these put away for
safe keeping; maybe some day she will give a few
of them to you.

As the days passed on, our outfit became as
one big family. Happy friendships were born and
live to this day.

We worked together, played together, sang
and drank together and when things were dark and
the going was rough, dirty and cruel, we stuck

together. Bill Doosey, dead now, was custodian and
master of the company's mascot, the accordion. It
came home with three service stripes.

Doosey was a big six-footer. In civil life
he was a traffic officer who guarded the busy
corner at Third and Market Streets, in
Philadelphia. How he could play! His big blue
Irish eyes would fairly dance out of their sockets
and his head swayed from side to side, keeping in
rhythm as his fingers rolled up and down the
keyboard of that music box.

There was Harp McDermott, the boiler maker,
who never did learn to pick up his step on the
march. He would hop up and down endlessly, trying
to get in step. Many a time McCormick would halt
the outfit, put his hands on his hips and yell,
"For --- --- sake, McDermott, do you have springs
in your shoes? You look like a jumping-jack on a
string." Buddy Eagle, our mechanic and official
chauffeur, was the hot-blooded boy of the outfit,
never wore a hat or overcoat. He was bawled out
more than any man in the outfit for careless
dress. It was a common sight to see Buddy running
around with laceless shoes, one puttee on, the
other dangling on the ground. His pockets bulging
with all sorts of paraphernalia, - screw drivers,
monkey wrenches, nuts, bolts, spark plugs, etc.,
he was really a walking machine shop. Despite his
appearance, Buddy was a mighty good mechanic and
rendered valuable service to the outfit. Bill
Lenox was the vocal entertainer. Upon the least
provocation, Bill would render anything from Sweet
Adeline to Rigoletto. Jim Roberts, from Fall
River, Mass., just a newly-wed, spent half his
time writing letters to his loved one and the
other half at the company post office, looking for
the answers. Slim Tyson could always be found, the
minute off duty, on his bunk, stretched on the
flat of his back, with arms in back of his head
and gazing skyward. Poor Dick Earnshaw was the
pessimist of the outfit. Dick hailed from
Washington D.C. He would sit on the end of his

bunk and stare at the floor for hours if someone
didn't break it up. Dick never expected to see
Washington again. Many a time, in one of these
trances, he would say, "Ah, I can see Pennsylvania
Avenue so plain, and how grand the dome of that
old capital looks." The fellows teased Dick a lot
and did all they could in bolstering his belief
that he was a marked man. "If I loved that old
dome as much as you do, I'd be damn proud to sleep
in Flanders field and let the poppies sprout from
my fertile soil," said Pat Marie, the humorist of
the gang. Dick would turn his head slowly and give
Pat a sickly look, rise slowly, and in his
southern drawl reply, "I don't think that's so --
----- funny, soldier," put his hands in his
pockets and stroll off to some quieter spot.

There was Joe Sherman, the official French
interpreter. The minute we landed Joe bought
himself a book called "Learn How to Speak French
in Thirty Days." Joe was the practical man of the
outfit. In a short time he was jabbering French
like a native and he knew the money system like
the Rothschilds. Joe never failed us when we asked
him to solve our French financial or domestic
problems.

Speaking about Joe, I think he was the
first man in the outfit sent to the guard house.
We were ordered on detail with the engineers one
day to clean out ditches at the side of a road
leading to St. Nazaire. It was a dirty job; water,
filth and slime had backed up until it was near
knee high. We were given shovels and told to get
busy. We jumped into this slime, but not Joe. The
officer in charge noticed him standing there,
resting on his shovel. "Well, soldier," he said
with a sarcastic flavor, "may I inquire why the
delay?" "I refuse to go into that ---- until I
have boots," was Joe's prompt reply. In a few
minutes we saw him marching up the road between an
honor guard with fixed bayonets. Joe accomplished
his point. He spent a few hours in the guard
house, but the next day we were issued boots.

Charlie Imhof was the statistician. He kept
his diary religiously, made an account of
everything that happened, checked over his
equipment once a week to see if anything was
missing, which was a good idea, because things did
seem to walk away at times.

I think I held the record for sleeping with
my hat and shoes on. I read a lot, always had a
book or magazine tucked under my bunk. I would
drop on my bunk and soon be deeply absorbed, often
going off and knowing nothing until the next
morning. The fellows would look at me and say,
"That guy must have been a fireman; there he is
again, all ready for the first alarm."

And so it went, all down the line; every
fellow had some little characteristic that
distinctly marked him and subjected him to a lot
of kidding. It was all done in a good-natured way
and accepted as such.

Army life is an excellent educator, as well
as a builder of muscle and body. It broadens your
mind and strengthens your character. Discipline is
a great leveler, it makes you lose that air of
self-importance and superiority that so easily
creeps into your system in civil life. You soon
learn to realize you are one of many gathered for
one objective. Each is assigned his individual
duty to arrive at that objective. At times it may
not be a pleasant duty and you may miss that
little word of encouragement you received in civil
life; but back of it all you have an inner tinge
of pride because you wear the uniform of your
country. You have been called to a high duty, and
in the exercise of that duty you learn how to take
it and hand it out. That's the fun of being a man,
as well as being alive.

Sunday afternoon was a great affair at
camp. The parade ground was turned into a huge
recreation center. Soccer, football, and baseball
games in any number. The weather was ideal. St.
Nazaire is situated in the southern portion of
France, and the weather in late November was like

our springs. The civilian population of the town
turned out in great numbers to watch our antics in
these various games. They were especially
interested in baseball, and it wasn't long before
they became as wild and noisy as our bleacher
fans. I think the Sunday afternoon visits did
those brave souls a world of good. They forgot for
the moment the heavy load they had been carrying
for three long years.

These French civilians told the price
France was paying in that conflict more clearly
than anything else. Almost all the women, old and
young, were in mourning. The few men in civilian
clothes carried the black band of death. No
family, it seemed, escaped the grim reaper of war.

Thanksgiving was a great day. We started at
eight o'clock on a hike to Pornichet, some eight
miles away. It is a little seashore resort, such
as you see in our country. The road from the camp
skirted the coast all the way out. In some spots
we were 100 feet above the water and one could see
for miles. A lighthouse was silhouetted against
the far horizon, and ships dotted the deep blue
surface of the sea as they ploughed their way to
and from the busy port. Seagulls by the hundreds
glided gracefully as they followed the wake of the
fishing smacks coming in from the fishing banks.
Tired and hungry, we returned to camp about 4:30.
Like a happy father, Tony was waiting for his
family.

We sat down to a real dinner -- turkey,
filling, cranberry jelly and everything that goes
with Thanksgiving, even to the mince pie. After
mess we visited the parade ground and listened to
the marine band. Toward evening, five or six of us
decided to go into town. Despite the good time the
day had brought, we were feeling a little low. It
was near the end of the month and francs were very
scarce among us. We walked around the town looking
at all the good things, but with little money to
spend. We passed a cafe were some fifteen French
soldiers were celebrating. That was too much for

Bill Doosey. He loved a drink and a good time.
Bill stopped and called a conference. We examined
our resources and found we could stand one drink
each. "Now listen, this is how we'll work it,"
said Bill in a whisper. "We'll order our drink and
get sort of acquainted with the boys, after that's
finished, we'll serenade them with the
Marseillaise. They'll be so tickled, nothing will
be too good for us. We'll hardly be able to walk
out of the place straight." We all agreed it was a
sound logic. So in we went. We were greeted with
open arms and before long we became one happy
family. So far Bill's idea was working a hundred
percent. We sang the Marseillaise with such
fervor, we almost brought tears to the eyes of the
little Frenchmen standing in back of the bar. When
the rendition was over, loud shouts echoed from
the walls, hats went into the air, people stopped
on the sidewalk to watch the demonstration. A
round of drinks was immediately ordered by the
Frenchmen for themselves, and two rounds for the
new-found heroes. Doosey's big eyes sparkled with
joy as he surveyed the two drinks sitting before
him. He settled down to what had all the
appearances of a jolly night. The holiday spirit
was in the air. Everything went along fine until I
noticed bottoms up with the Frenchmen and we were
still sipping our second. Were they looking for
the rich Americans to return the treat?

Presently the whole place came to
attention, and the strains of the Star Spangled
Banner swept softly through the smoky air. I
looked at Doosey and he was already backing to the
exit. At the final chord we were out of the door.
As we ran up the street there were loud shouts
from the Frenchmen standing on the sidewalk. What
they said I don't know, but I doubt if it was
complimentary. That was probably the first and
last time the American army ever retreated on
French soil. On our way to camp, Doosey spoke up.
"That was a dam swell idea, the only thing I
forgot about was the Star Spangled Banner." A few

days later we received our first pay in France. We
met our friends this time on an equal footing. We
had a grand time and the American army was
redeemed once more.

A bright crisp day in early December found
us at the station of St. Nazaire bound for
Bourmont in Northern France. It was like leaving
home as we slipped away from this delightful
seaport town. We had been there just a little over
a month, yet it seemed as if I had known the place
all my life. We traveled in the third-class
coaches. They were entirely different from our
coaches, having a small corridor on one side and
divided up in little compartments. We had an
opportunity to see a great deal of France on our
four days' journey northbound. France is very
proud of her farm lands and forests. For miles
every bit of land was under cultivation. Women
were busy working in the fields, children dropped
their baskets and waved to us as we rattled by.

The cattle roamed lazily between boundary
lines of stone walls that separated the farms.
These walls extended for miles; at times they
looked like little rivulets of water winding their
way in the most fantastic curves over the rolling
countryside. In the distance you could see a
little hamlet, with the red tile roofs and the
village church steeple peeping at you from behind
openings in the foliage of the forests. Standing
on a hill like a lone sentinel of the ages, a
chateau would appear, with dull gray towers
silhouetted against the sky. It seemed hard to
believe, amid this peaceful landscape that God had
made so beautiful, that we were journeying to the
land of desolation where hamlets were nothing but
heaps of broken stone, and stumps of scarred wood
stood where forests one lived.

Bourmont and Goncourt

We arrived at Bourmont just as the sun was rising above the eastern hills. It was a small hamlet situated in a little valley along the Meuse, about twenty miles south of Neufchateau, on the main rail line to Toul and Nancy. Bourmont was a quaint village, consisting of one street running at right angles to the railway.

To the right of the tracks, the road followed the steep grade of the slope, extending for perhaps two miles to the summit. Here an old chateau stood in close company with the village church. Many times in the early spring we took a pilgrimage to this beautiful spot and looked down upon the valley and across the hills. To the left of the tracks, the main part of the village centered. It was flat but very picturesque, as the Meuse twisted in graceful curves under the old stone bridges and pathways that traversed the village.

It was very cold when we arrived here; the trees were bare of leaves, and everything took on the appearance of real winter.

We marched about four miles along a beautiful winding limestone road, lined with trees, that followed the river.

Finally we halted at a little side path that led to an old chateau, situated on the hill some half a mile off the main road.

It stood alone, surrounded by big evergreens and pines. They told us it was five hundred years old, and had been the home of a wealthy land-owner of long ago. Now it was the most dilapidated place you ever saw. It was built of gray stone. The window frames were entirely gone, rough pine boards covered the openings, many

tiles in the roof were missing, and big patches of
tin and paper covered the surface.

At the rear was the old bathing pool, with
fragments of waterlily plants still clinging to
the slimy stone, parts of the limestone coping
still existed and broken steps that led to the
ancient sunken garden were still in evidence.

Fragments of statuary were scattered about,
as if trying to cling to the splendor of times
along since past. This was to be our new home. We
passed Christmas here, and saw the dawn of the New
Year, come rising over the hills. Within the
shelter of the gray stone walls and the warmth of
the roaring flames in the huge fireplace, we spent
the cold winter days and nights of 1917 and 1918.

Many nights I lay on my bunk and gazed at
the barren walls that enclosed me. I could picture
oil paintings in gilded frames hanging from the
heavy cornics mould, richly carved furniture
cushioned on thick orientals, a child with long
tresses hanging across her shoulders sitting at
the piano, bringing to life the soft notes from
the works of the great masters, while Mother and
Dad reclined in heavy upholstered chairs under the
soft glow from the glass spangled chandelier that
hung from the ceiling.

Time does carry changes. Each hour ticks
away, never to return. To every hour life is
created within us, and as it passes we have only
the memories of what it brought. We can never call
them back; they pass as a shooting star crosses
the heavens and fades beyond the distant horizon.

We established our kitchen on the first
floor, and decided to use the second and third
floors for sleeping quarters. In the front room of
the second floor was a huge fireplace where most
of us settled. Lieut McCormick, Jerry Mulhern, and
a few other, took the rear room. Our Captain
decided to take a room in a private home in the
hamlet of Goncourt, about a mile north. Life took
on a different aspect now. For the first time we
were alone -- no more camp life, no more mingling

with the mass of troops we were accustomed to,
just the quiet atmosphere of our own surroundings.
We were not entirely alone, however, as part of
the Second Division was billeted around Goncourt.

It wasn't long before we adjusted ourselves
to the new life before us. Squad details were
formed, one digging latrines and policing, another
going to the forest to cut wood for the winter
supply, others going to the railroad station to
unload supplies.

We had long hikes with full pack over the
snowy fields and through thick forests, to harden
us. We had gas-mask drills, and target practice
with our 45 automatics. The long nights were spent
around the huge fireplace, with the big logs
crackling merrily and giving off a golden glow
that cast soft shadows around the room.

I can see the old gang now: some writing
letters to loved ones at home, others playing
cards, others sitting on boxes watching the flames
dancing and curling up the chimney, while others
lay on their bunks gazing at the ceiling, absorbed
in their own thoughts.

Some nights we would walk down to the
village of Goncourt and get a glass of beer in the
village cafe. It was a neat little place with a
small pine bar at one side. On the wall in back of
the bar were old French prints that had been in
the family for years. A small stove was off to one
corner. Little pine tables and benches were
scattered about. The proprietor was a chubby
little red-faced man; his wife was a neat little
woman, always wearing a velvet band tied tightly
around her neck.

They had a daughter, Yvonne, a charming
little lady about twenty-one. She had long golden
hair, - she was rare indeed, as most of the French
girls had dark hair. She was very shy and usually
sat near the stove, knitting. Once in a while a
little curl would cover her lips and she would
drop her knitting and listen to us as we sang the
old army airs. Each visit found me glancing in the

direction of Yvonne more and more. I also noticed
my glances were being returned; a little curl of
the mouth turned into an open smile.

I wasn't alone in attentions going Yvonne's
way. Pretty soon it developed into an open race. I
never had a steady girl in the States. I knew a
few, of course, but it never got more serious than
an occasional visit to a show or romping around
with the gang at the shore. Now I found a tiny
tinge of jealousy creeping over me whenever any of
the boys shoed an over-abundance of affection for
this little Mademoiselle.

One night we were all having a good time. A
fellow attached to a machine gun company of the
Second Division was feeling a little gay; he made
advances to her. She resented it very much, ran
over to the corner where I was sitting, and sat
beside me. Every visit after that found Yvonne at
my side. We struck up a happy friendship. She
attended school in Neufchateau and spoke and
understood English quite well. I told her about
our great country. She talked about New York, of
its wonderful parks, people, theatres, public
buildings and skyscrapers, like one who had
visited there. I asked her one day how she came to
know this city so well. She jumped up, ran into
the dining room and returned with a big book that
contained pictures of nearly every building in the
city. "You see, I am a typical New Yorker."

She told me the story of France as only a
native child could, of the misery and heart-aches
the last three years had brought. Uncles and
cousins that went away, never to return. "Yes,
this small hamlet," with tears streaming down her
pale cheeks, "like thousands of others, spread
over our blessed countryside, knows what it is to
suffer. Wars are cruel and heartless, yet it seems
France must have them just to live. Maybe perhaps,
you and your brave comrades will finish for all
time this thing called war, and let me and France
live in peace, eh?"

As the days went by, we paid frequent
visits to the cafe. Yvonne became the symbol of
that three-thousand-mile trek across the ocean. To
me she represented every hamlet, every peasant,
every stream and river, everything that was good
and noble in the stricken country. Her philosophy
of life was so simple; she asked for very little,
she had not been spoiled by riches nor the lavish
layout of fine clothes nor the idle affections of
wise men. To live in the humble surroundings of
her little hamlet in peace was the only thing she
desired.

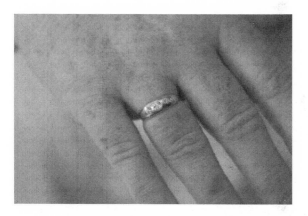

Before leaving home, Nanna gave me a ring
of hers to wear. It had three little diamond
chips. On our way up the hill one Sunday morning
to the little village church, I slipped the ring
onto her finger. "Here, you take care of this for
me. It belongs to my mother, and with the rough
life of soldiering I am afraid something may
happen to it."
"Oh no, I can't do this, " she said.
"Suppose you get orders to leave in a minute," she
shrugged her shoulders. "No ring, what then, eh?"
I assured her if that happened I would come back
for it sometime.

She wore the ring many months. I traveled many miles through France and saw much of this thing called war, as she described it, before I again put the ring on my finger.

The winter at Goncourt was very cold, and with it came plenty of snow. The wind whistled through the big evergreens surrounding the chateau, in what seemed like endless days.

For weeks the countryside wore a mantle of white, and trees crackled and groaned under the weight of snow and ice. It was all very beautiful, just like the snow scenes you see so much in your Christmas cards.

Time, however, passes swiftly on, and Spring broke fast upon us in early March. Old men, women and youngsters began to dot the fields. Cows and sheep were driven to the open spaces. Birds began to herald the coming dawn, and the old heavy woolens began to feel itchy. We all felt like youngsters on the first days of summer vacation. Balls, bats and gloves were resurrected from beneath the bunks. Even the old swimming pool was put to use by some of the hardy boys. We took on more intensive training, consisting of hikes to surrounding hamlets and long hours of drilling and target practice.

We visited the village of Gondrecourt, some eight miles away, where the 1st Division was in training, to see General Pershing review the troops before they left for the St. Mihiel sector. We also saw him review the Second Division at Goncourt. He was a fine looking soldier, stepping with the grace of a thoroughbred being led to the track.

One fine Saturday morning, we asked Top Sergeant Butcher to ask Lieut. McCormick if he would excuse us from the old army routine and allow us to choose sides for a good game of ball. The sun was bright, not a cloud in the sky, and a gently breeze came up from the south. To our delight, he fell in line, and soon we were all on the field, including the Lieutenant, having a

swell time. Soon we saw our Captain coming up the
road. He walked across the field. "Lieutenant," he
shouted, and we all came to attention. "Assemble
the men for a full day hike. You will arrive back
for mess at 5:30. Men will march with full pack,
raincoats, and gum boots."

We paid dearly for our few minutes of
enjoyment. All along the march, soldier and people
alike stared at us, then bursted out laughing. To
us it was not so funny. When we got back that
afternoon our feet were sore, you can believe me.

It seems a West Pointer who was in command
of a machine gun battalion, was walking up the
road and saw us playing ball. He happened to meet
our Captain on the road and bawled him out for
lack of discipline and setting a bad example to
the rest of the troops billeted in the vicinity.
He had had a couple of tilts with this officer
before, and he was furious all the way through.

We had plenty of discipline for the next
couple of weeks. Every little slip carried extra
duty of some kind. The following Monday he spotted
me at reveille with a button not closed over one
of the pockets of my blouse. I was put on K.P.
duty for two weeks. One night around eleven
o'clock I was awakened from a sound sleep. Tony,
the cook, was standing over me. "Come on
downstairs, I want you to look at those pans you
washed tonight." I slowly pulled myself together
and followed him down the rickety stairs. He
rubbed his finger across the pans. You could
clearly see plenty of grease as evidence of a bum
job. "How would you like to eat stuff out of pans
like that?" I made the excuse that the water was
cold when I washed them. "Well, here you are,
plenty of hot water. Get busy." There was nothing
much to do except roll up my sleeves and get
going.

At Reveille and Retreat the Captain usually
gave us a little talk on the qualities of being a
good soldier, or some discourse on army life. He
always ended up by saying, "Thank you, men, for

your kind attention. Lieutenant, dismiss the
Company." One evening we were assembled for
retreat. The Captain gave his usual talk and ended
with his "Thank you, men, for your kind
attention." "The same to you, you big bum!" came
out of the air. The Captain stopped. "Will the man
who said that have the courage to step out of line
and come forward?" No one moved. Finally he and
the Lieutenant polled every man. No one admitted
he was the guilty person. There upon the Captain
gave orders for no one to leave the premises for
two weeks.

After we were dismissed, we started to
inquire who the culprit was that brought this
trouble on the entire company. One fellow in the
rear rank said he was sure it came from the
boarded-up window at the kitchen wall, directly in
back of where we were assembled. We immediately
investigated and found that the two K.P.'s had had
an argument. It seems one fellow said, "Merry
Christmas, potato peeler," and the other one
retorted with the now famous saying, "The same to
you, you big bum." It was timed right to the
second. The Lieutenant had a hard job convincing
the Captain this was the true version of the
affair; nevertheless he relented, and we were all
pardoned.

He was a very peculiar man, and very
erratic at times. One day I was walking down the
road with him. About half a mile away we saw
someone approaching. As he got a little closer, we
could see he was an officer. The Captain
immediately took his hands out of his inner coat
pocket, buttoned his overcoat and ordered me three
paces behind. There we marched, I trailing three
paces behind, while he gave me a lesson on army
regulations. Presently we passed the officer, who
happened to be a Second Lieutenant. The Captain
called me alongside of him again. "Damn it, just a
shave-tail. He looked for all the world like that
West Pointer who commands the machine gun

battalion." He was taking no chances on getting
bawled out again.

One morning in late March, a dispatch rider
on a motorcycle swung off the main road and up the
lane. He was covered with the white powdered dust
of the limestone roads. He reached into his
leather pouch, brought out a large envelope and
handed it to Lieut. McCormick. That night we were
advised of its contents, - off to the front.

We were to split up. Lieut. McCormick was
to take ten men under his command, to be known as
Advance Group No. 1, and proceed to Menil-la-Tour,
about seven miles behind the trenches on the St.
Mihiel front, known as the Toul sector. Our
Captain was to take the remainder of the company
and proceed to Soissons. He told us that Advance
Group No. 1 would go on duty in the lines, working
with the First Division, who had been in active
service for some time. He also advised us
McCormick would pick his own men and let them know
in the morning.

The atmosphere was mighty blue around the
old Chateau that night. We had all become pretty
much attached, and there was never any inkling
that the unit would be separated. We had been
together now about six months, and a better gang
could not have been assembled under one roof. They
came from all walks of life: cops, firemen,
architects, engineers, undertakers, clerks,
mechanics, chauffeurs, one divinity student, and a
quiet, studious New Englander from Harvard. Surely
it represented Democracy in the best form.

It was a tough blow, but what could we do
about it? Someone started the old reliable, "We're
in the army now." After the rendition, we headed
for the village cafe, and there, amid song and
laughter, soon forgot our troubles. I tried to
keep away from Yvonne that night, but it wasn't
long before she was sitting beside me. "You are
going away, eh?" she said quietly. I laughed it
off. "Why worry now? We have another night left to
talk that over. Let's have a good time." I bade

her goodbye that night and did not see her again
for many months. I thought of her many times. In
the course of my travels, I visited many French
homes and met many French people, but, somehow or
other, she still seemed to represent all that was
good in France.

The following morning the personnel of
McCormick's group was announced. Your Uncle Jim
and I were among them, together with Doosey,
Mulhern, La Rue, Anismen, Tyson, McDermott,
Keating and Murphy. We were to leave early the
following morning, the rest of the company leaving
later the same day.

That evening, McCormick came into the room
with two large boxes. They contained bullets. We
were ordered to load automatics, and received a
reserve supply for our cartridge belts. War was
coming closer. It was a sickening feeling for the
moment, I give you my word. But someone always
slipped into the picture to ease the burden. Pat
Marie spoke up and said, "Well, Dick, I can still
see that old dome in Washington, but believe me,
the mist is getting thicker all the time." Dick
never said a word, just kept on putting the
bullets into the automatic case, one by one.

It was a wild night. No one slept. We
emptied the straw from our bed sacks and dumped it
into the fireplace. After that we took the bunks,
broke them up, and in they went. After that, the
boarding that closed the window openings went in.
All night long the blaze continued. Laughter and
song to the strains of our accordion rocked the
barren walls. It was our last fling together, and
here, amid the lone guard of the majestic
evergreens and pines.

"The night [to paraphrase Longfellow's words]
Was filed with music,
And the cares that infested the day,
Shall fold their tents, like the Arabs,
And silently steal away."

Off to the Front

At seven o'clock the next morning we were
off to the little railroad station tucked in the
hills on the outskirts of Goncourt. Sometime
around noon we arrived at Toul. Here we got our
first glimpse of combat, anti-aircraft guns
situated high on the hill were barking at an enemy
plane. A few hours later we were traveling on a
little narrow gauge railroad that ran along the
side of the road leading to Menil-la-Tour. The
little cars or trucks that carried us were the
darnedest things you ever saw. They were about
five feet long, with iron sides about four feet
high. Each truck carried about six men. The tiny
engine chugged and snorted until you thought it
was going to push its sides out and crumble to
pieces. The ride was noisy, jumpy and very lonely.
We say very few civilians. Big army trucks,
ammunition wagons and motorcycles raced up and
down the road.

As we continued, we could see fortification
mounds for gun emplacements here and there.
Somehow or other it began to look cold and dreary.
Weeds were growing in the fields, big patches of
stone walls were broken through. The wide open
spaces looked lonely, with no sign of cattle
grazing anywhere. We arrived in Menil-la-Tour
about disk. We were tired, dirty, and hungry.
McCormick immediately went to the billeting
officer to get quarters for us, but there were
none to be had. The only place available was in
the hay loft of an old barn on the outskirts of
the village. It didn't make much difference to us
where we slept. The important thing just then was
eats.

After a good hot meal of beef stew and a
scrub at the horse trough, we ambled on down to

our new quarters, climbed the ladder to the
hayloft, covered ourselves over with blankets and
hay, and went to sleep. Sometime during the night
I was awakened by a heavy report, and then
another. The sides of the old barn vibrated. I
thought at first it was a thunderstorm
approaching. It was not long, however, before I
realized what it was. The reports became more
frequent until it seemed like one huge rolling
peal of thunder. Every once in a while you could
hear a distinct thud, with a peculiar shudder. How
long the barrage lasted I don't know. I remembered
no more until I heard Joe Anisman yell. I stuck my
head from under the hay. It was daylight, and
there standing before me was an old French soldier
with a pitchfork in his hand. He did not realized
he had received visitors during the night. Joe
told me he yelled to him just as he was about to
dig in for a load of hay directly over me.

Coming from the quiet hills of Goncourt to
this place with all its confusion was a distinct
change: troops by the hundreds, officers darting
around inside cars and automobiles, big gray
trucks thundering along with all sorts of
supplies; mules and horses dragging their
instruments of war over muddy fields. It took on a
real military aspect. We knew now that we were in
the theatre of war.

A little to the north of the village,
soldiers were unloading shells by the thousands
from ammunition trucks and piling them neatly over
a place covering perhaps five or six acres. These
places were known as ammunition dumps. They were
scattered around and located in secluded spots and
cleverly camouflaged so the enemy could not spot
them from the air. Most of the unloading and
activity around these important reserve dumps was
done under cover of darkness, because every day
enemy observation planes were coming over looking
for unusual movements or concentration of troops.
A month or so later, however, a German observer
located the position of this dump. Direct hits

were made and for a while it sounded as if hell let loose. You could see the glow for miles, and the earth quivered as thousands of shells exploded.

Barbed wire entanglements were being constructed and men were busy digging trenches. New American Divisions were moving up constantly, and the French were moving west to help stem the tide of the great German horde about to move in the direction of Paris.

German troops were being concentrated around the railhead at Metz, and all through the Alsace-Lorraine sector, which led us to believe the Germans were getting ready to drive on St. Mihiel and on through to Toul and Nancy. More reserve troops were brought up from the rear and every hamlet for miles around was loaded with American troops. Things looked so desperate in the Spring that divisions fresh from the transports were shipped direct to reserve positions in back of the lines, instead of having short training periods in the interior, as had been the custom.

There must have been close to 500,000 men called in reserved positions by late Spring; so different from the little band of men when we arrived in St. Nazaire. We began to feel like old veterans. The boys coming over now were full of pep. We plied them with questions about home, how camp life was over there, and how they liked soldiering. There were a good-looking bunch of youngsters. Their skin,however, looked a little washy in contrast to the deep tan we had acquired from the winds of Goncourt.

We stayed in Menil-la-Tour about a week, and then moved to Sebastopol, a short distance away, where Evacuation Hospital No. 1 was located. Before the war this had been an army outpost consisting of several one story brick buildings with limestone trimmings. It was now the scene of much activity. The wounded were brought in from the first aid stations. The serious cases were treated there and then moved on back to the base hospitals.

About two miles east of the hospital, the 94th Aero Squadron was located. Many of its members consisted of the famous Lafayette Escadrille. Major Maoul Lufberry, the American ace, was in command. One day he swept into the skies from the air field to meet a lone enemy plane circling high overhead, never to return again. Eddie Rickenbacker, another famous ace, made his death-dealing flights from this field.

We were assigned to a squad tent. Summer was in the offing and that looked good to us. A promotion, certainly, from the hayloft at Menil-la-Tour. Action on the front was increasing and death was beginning to take its toll. I had my first job of plotting a cemetery just beyond Menil-la-Tour, located on a sloping piece of ground just off the road, planned to hold 500 men. A big center plot was reserved for grass and flowers, with a flag pole being the focal point. As I worked on this bare piece of ground with my tape and lines, marking off the walks and burial plots, I sincerely hoped a miracle or something would happen to make the completion of this ghastly job impossible. My hopes never reached reality. Every day brought new crosses, and before I left to go into the Argonne the little village cemetery of Menil-la-Tour had fulfilled its mission. This was, I believe, the first American cemetery plotted for men who died in action. Later on I was to plot the first and the most advanced American cemetery on the lines.

One week after we arrived at Sebastopol, we received a Ford truck. One morning shortly after, McCormick said, "Well, boys, side arms, helmets and gas masks; we're off to Mandres." We had heard about this village, situated directly to the rear of the trenches; now we were to see it. We loaded the truck with wooden crosses, metal plates and the stenciling outfit. Lieut. McCormick carried the record slips. A record was made of the

soldier's name, his serial number, rank, outfit,
where he was killed, and the date of death. Later
on, when the troops advanced, we carried a
military map of the sector, laid out and
coordinated into kilometer squares. These maps
were very complete; every road, stream, farm
house, barn, forest, and even clump of trees was
spotted accurately to scale. When we spotted
graves in the field or buried in shell holes, we
could easily determine the square on the map and
by coordination locate them to within a definite
degree of accuracy. This coordination location was
put on their record slip. These records were sent
to headquarters at Chaumont, and in that way a
complete check was had on every man killed and
almost the exact spot where his body could be
found. Later on the isolated and scattered groups
of bodies were put into larger plots and finally
transferred to the permanent American cemeteries.

Close to the Trenches

Our little truck swung out on the lane from
the hospital and onto the main road. We passed
Menil-la-Tour. Our eyes were wide open, surveying
the new country, but not much was said. We were
wondering (at least I was) what it was like up
there. Pretty soon it became very lonesome and
drab. Here and there you would see a few soldiers
appearing as if coming from nowhere. A little
further on, glimpses of artillery locations with
men walking around and completely hidden from
above by shrubs and branches of trees. Barbed wire
was stretched in zigzag lines, extending, it
seemed, till it touched the horizon, shell holes
dotted the fields, villages deserted except for a
few soldiers poking their heads above the ground,
great holes in walls that refused to go down,
roofs with bending curves that reached to the
basement, huge chunks of masonry and debris
scattered everywhere.

We now began to pass between patches of
camouflage, lined on each side of the road. This
was where the elevation was highest and could be
seen from the German Observation Balloons. About a
mile and one half from Mandres we were stopped by
an M.P. guarding the road. This was the outpost
for travel during the day if action was heavy. He
asked to see McCormick's credentials, and looked
them over carefully. He glanced into the truck to
see what we had. McCormick started to kid him.
"Well, Lieutenant, it's serious business up here.
We take nothing for granted." He then related a
story told to him when the French held the lines
here.

A farmer who owned a small herd of cows
refused to leave the danger zone. He said he had

lived there a great many years, and saw no reason
to leave. He was willing to take his chances, as
he described it. Finally the military authorities
left him alone. After a time things were not going
so good. Every move the French made seemed to be
known by the enemy. As soon as fresh troops were
in the trenches, a surprise attack was launched to
smash morale; new artillery locations were
shelled. There was a leak somewhere along the
line. Suspicion finally centered on the farmer.
They looked over his herd and found they all
varied in color, and some were noticeably spotted.
They also observed that on few occasions was the
entire herd out at one time -- usually two or
three would be out at a time, and they varied in
color and spot combination every day. It was not
long before they had the solution: a code system
was in operation between the farmer and the German
Sausage Balloon, where observers with powerful
glasses watched the combinations and knew every
move made by the French.

Mandres

McCormick asked if we could proceed. The
M.P. said he didn't think we would run into any
trouble, as it had been the quietest day of the
week; but he cautioned us to be careful and put on
speed at a turn in the road some half mile up. It
was known as "Dead Man's Curve" and the Germans
had an accurate range on it. "In fact," he said,
"the only action today occurred there early this
morning before daylight." The M.P. was right -- it
was pockmarked with shell holes on both sides; as
grim evidence we saw one horse in the ditch and
what looked like a two-wheeled cart blown to bits.
We arrived in the village of Mandres.
Outside of a few battered walls still standing and
great mounds of crumbled masonry, there wasn't
much to be seen. A portion of the village church
and part of the roof was still intact, but jagged
holes showed where shells had gone through. The
stone tower was completely blown away. We visited
the little battle-scarred French cemetery in back
of the church, stamped the names of the men on the
plates and put the wooden crosses on the fresh
mounds of our comrades. There were about twenty-
five or thirty here at this time. If the roads
were under heavy shell-fire they were buried here,
and when conditions warranted they were carried
back to the cemetery at Menil-la-Tour.
Well, here we were at the front. We could
see the ruined village of Seicheprey and the
ridges of the trenches a short distance in front
of us. Barbed wire entanglements seemed to be
running in all directions. The ground looked like
the surface of a lake dented by big drops of rain.
Directly to the rear of the church were perhaps a
dozen light artillery dugouts stretching out for

some distance. The guns were entirely underground,
with the end of the barrels protruding above the
ground. Machine gun nests were located within the
battered ruins of the village and yet with all
these instruments of destruction so close to us
there was absolute silence -- a dead silence I
never experienced before.

It seemed as if everything was waiting --
standing still lest the sound of a breath send the
universe to eternity. The chirp of a bird, the hum
of a bee, yes, even the gnawing of a rat would
have been a welcome sound. I was up there many
times after, when the guns were barking and men
with wings spat fire from high in the heavens; but
I never again experienced the horror of my first
trip. Truly it was the land of nowhere!

We completed our work, and soon were
turning Dead Man's Curve on our way home. We were
about two miles south of Mandres when we heard a
couple of dull thuds to the east. Clouds of thick
yellowish smoke were rolling lazily along close to
the ground. We found later it was the beginning of
a severe gas attack that lasted well into the
following morning.

That night as I stretched on my bunk I
could hear the rolling of the drums. From under
the side flaps of the tent I could see flashes
along the northern horizon that resembled sheet
lightning dancing through the clouds at the close
of a hot summer day. Brighter lights of various
colors mingled as signal flares shot into the sky.
The land of nowhere had come to life. The sleeping
instruments of destruction of a few hours ago had
awakened and were growling and spitting amid that
village that knew no peace. The horror of silence,
then the weird moans of cannons, the shrieking
whistle of shells as they sped through the air,
the shudder as particles of earth mixed with hot
shrapnel flew high above the tree-tops. Surely God
never created a land like that!

It is not my intention, Sashie, to fill
your little mind with all the dark things of life.

I would like to see you get all the good things
that life offers, and there are many. But we
cannot afford to be sentimental or cast realities
aside. Dark shadows do fall across our path as we
travel through life. You will pass through them,
and you will be called upon to share in carrying
the burden of your times. As this story unravels
and the cobwebs from the brain cells of twenty or
more years are broken, I cannot help but feel that
the deep shadows they knew so well are with us
again.

The great sore was opened in 1914. Pus
flowed for four long years, and we thought the
wound had been healed, but the seepage continued;
and as I write this little story for you now in
1940 the flow has increased -- yes, in some
respects worse than the times I relate to you. It
will be to your generation and to those you bear
to guard against this cancerous flow.

Our boys who rest beneath the scattered
soil of France, wearing the uniform of the country
they loved, call to you, but they are not
beckoning us to come and share the strange soil of
distant lands where they are resting. They must
wonder at times at the similarity of the fine and
noble phrases of twenty-three years ago, that
carried them across the sea, and their
resurrection again today.

They see history repeating as surely as the
sun will rise again from the darkness of the night
to shine upon the hollow ground above them. They
watch in silence the skeletons of 1914 to 1918,
awakened from their long slumber, dusted off and
dressed again in noble motives for the salvation
of mankind.

They heard all this long ago. They died
that Democracy might live throughout the world,
that no more should War Lords, crazed with power
and the lust for blood, march against
civilization. They, the dead, have fulfilled their
mission, but we, the living, somewhere along the
line have failed miserable to carry on. They might

well ask, why the spirit of Democracy has faded
faster since the signing of the Versailles Treaty
than in any like period of our times, and why
leaders more wicked and bloodthirsty than the ones
they knew, were all allowed to become powerful
enough to throw the world into gasping convulsions
of horror again.

These are difficult questions for us to
answer, but nevertheless the picture stands before
us in the stark nakedness of reality. We must
defend our free institutions and our liberties
with all we have and lend a helping hand to those
nations who want to live in peace; but if there
ever comes a time again when our youth must fight
in the defense of Democracy, let them fall on the
soil where true Democracy was born.

We traveled far, twenty-three years ago, to
make the world safe for Democracy. We are at the
cross-roads now. We can stay within our own shores
or we can again set sail for the uncharted waters
of intrigue and hate, where we will see again the
mirage of a towering Utopia rising from the mist.
With hands dripping with blood we will grasp at it
for a time. We will set our course westward again
and the rain and the snow will fall from strange
skies upon rows of new crosses of the ones we
leave behind -- and then -- who knows? Twenty-five
years hence youngsters yet unborn will trim sails
again to embark on this mission of
disillusionment.

We can assume this position in the universe
until we become so weakened physically, morally
and economically that the very principles we
sacrificed so much to preserve may be caught in
the whirlpool of intrigue and lost to us forever.

Toul

The city of Toul lies about six or seven miles south of Sebastopol. We made many visits to this historic town. It is one of the middle-sized cities of France. To the north, in the direction of Alsace-Lorraine, it was protected by a huge earthen mound, rising some two hundred feet. Artillery fortifications were spotted along the slopes. On the extreme top anti-aircraft guns protected the city from air raids. Like all French cities, it had beautiful parks and public buildings. The cobbled stone streets were narrow, winding through the town like small streams. Soldiers sipped their wine on the sidewalks under the shade of brightly colored awnings. Big plants of evergreens and palms in huge green buckets were scattered between the marble-covered tables. Far off in the corner, an old Frenchman with flowing white beard, wearing a polka-dot scarf tucked into a worn velvet coat, played a violin, keeping time with the tap of his wooden shoes against the flagstone terrace.

French officers in their tailor-made uniforms promenading with smartly dressed Mademoiselles. Girls and boys on bicycles, carrying bundles in wire baskets attached to the handle bars. Two-wheel carts rattling over the cobblestone roads, carrying all sorts of things, driven by old Grandpa with his grandson perched on top. Fountains spitting water, with youngsters splashing at each other, American officers and soldiers, some without and others with a Mademoiselle, strutting along gaily, arm in arm. Cafes with soldiers standing at the bar, and thick clouds of cigarette smoke curling to the ceiling,

some dancing with chic Mademoiselles sweeping in
graceful spins to the tune of a player piano;
others munching over a plate of ham and eggs.
Official army cars with Generals, Colonels and
Majors, weaving through traffic. U.S. Marines
assigned as Military Police with side arms and
stick, parading the streets. Soldiers in the
Y.M.C.A., K. of C. and S.A. rooms, writing
letters, reading magazines, and sipping hot
chocolate. All this was Toul. Soldiers on leave in
the gay atmosphere of holiday spirit.

Our first visit to Toul was in search of a
good hot bath in a tub, where we could just wallow
around and soak for an hour or more. We had been
in France some time now, and a good scrub was
rare.

We inquired of a little French youngster
where the bath house was. He didn't understand. We
made all sorts of gestures. Finally he understood.
"Ah, oui," his face lit up. "Bains, bains, Oui,
oui, Monsieur." He led us to a building that
looked more like a public library than a bathing
house. It was quite ornate, with a formal court, a
bed of flowers and fountain in the center and
evergreens and shrubbery bordered the flagstone
walks.

The little bathing rooms, about ten by ten
feet, framed around the court. You registered in
the large lobby, then received the number of your
room and paid your bill. I believe it was about
fifty cents. You then waited for the lady
attendant to assign you to a room. She scrubbed
the tub, gave you soap and a towel. "Does Monsieur
desire back washed?" she asked as I entered my
room. "Anything extra?" I smiled. "No, no,
Monsieur, that is part of service. Frenchmen all
have back washed." I told her I thought I could
take care of my own back, so I was left all alone
to soak to my heart's content.

When we got together again Doosey rubbed
his hands. "Boys, from now on a bath twice a week
whether I need it or not. You know -- this army

life's not so bad after all." You could easily
guess. Bill had his back washed.

Warming Up

Action increased along the front and the wounded where coming in fast with the natural percentages of casualties. I plotted a hospital cemetery about a quarter of a mile away from the buildings. It was here that Major Lufberry was buried, together with many more of his comrades who died fighting in the air.

Our trips to Mandres and Seicheprey were more frequent now, but we never struck a day like our first trip again. Frequently we had to stop at the outpost and walk up the road, spread at ten paces apart. To see shells bursting and throwing great clouds of dirt was no longer new. Planes sweeping across the sky in deadly combat was a frequent occurrence. One day we saw three observation balloons come down in flames in less than ten minutes. Another day, walking up the road, we noticed a German plane flying low. As he approached we made for the ditch and threw ourselves down. He made a dive and opened his gun. Little particles of dust rose from the road about fifty feet ahead of us. Fortunately for us, his dive wasn't sharp enough.

Another day, a Mosquito ambulance left Mandres, while we were there, with two wounded boys. A half an hour later a courier on motorcycle arrived in the village and told us that two miles down the road an ambulance had been blown off the road, killing the two wounded men and the driver. On our way down we stopped to investigate. A shell had hit directly on the road; there was a gaping hole in the side of the ambulance, and the force of the explosion must have lifted it clear off the ground, because it had crossed the ditch and was lying in the field.

Scattered about in the wreckage, I noticed a blood soaked piece of paper. I picked it up. It was a letter on Y.M.C.A. stationery. It read:

"My dearest Mother,
I am a real soldier now. I am in the front lines and very close to the enemy. It's not so bad during the day but the nights are not so good. Somehow I feel protected though up here because everybody's in dugouts or trenches. We never hardly stick our head out of the ground.
Eddie is with me, and it don't..."

That was all I could make out -- the rest was bloodstained.

I destroyed the letter, because I had no desire to carry such grim evidence around with me, but I did record the last words of some youngster to his mother.

The boys on the Soissons front were gaining in experience also. We received word that ten or twelve of them had a narrow escape. They were pacing up the road under shell fire. Directly ahead of them were two French kitchen wagons and a detachment of French soldiers. A shell hit directly on the road, smashed the wagons to bits and killed and wounded a number of French. Our fellows were knocked down by the concussion, but outside of being spattered with dirt came off O.K.

The First Major Skirmish

Toward the end of April, the first division holding the lines on the St. Mihiel front was called by Marshal Foch to go into action on the ridge of Montdidier beyond Cantigny and covering the Paris-Calais railway. They were relieved by the 26th Yankee division from Massachusetts under command of General Edwards.

The 26th engaged in the first major skirmish of the A.E.F. They were just about settled in the lines when the Germans launched a surprise attack during the night. They opened a deadly barrage and then stormed the trenches in waves. It was the most violent attack so far launched against the American troops. Our casualties numbered around nine hundred, with a hundred and fifty or more killed. The Germans also captured a hundred and eighty-three prisoners.

In the early morning our troops left the trenches and made a counter attack upon the German lines, inflicting heavy casualties all along the line. The barrage started to roll about eleven o'clock at night. Sharp flashes swept across the sky. The noise was terrific. It lasted all night, and was still going heavy when McCormick saw us at breakfast. "There's hell up the line. We're ordered up right away -- report after you finish your eats." We knew there was trouble -- ambulances and trucks with the wounded were coming in thick. It looked like messy business ahead. All the way up the road the roll became louder and louder. Planes were looping and diving at each other. About two and a half miles out from Mandres an officer came running across the field, holding up his hand for us to stop. I never before saw such a forlorn looking creature. He was caked with

mud, one leg of his breeches was hanging in
shreds, his eyes were red and swollen. He asked
where we were going. When we told him Mandres, his
face lighted up. "Good! My battery's up there and
out of ammunition, poor devils. I have three cases
over here. Let's get busy and load them on."
     The cases, as I remember them, were of
iron, about two feet by three feet and about
eighteen or twenty inches high. It took about four
of us to lift one case. When we loaded it on the
truck the old springs touched the axle. McCormick
looked at our little truck and shook his head.
"Sorry, old man, that's the best we can do this
trip." We were just about to start off when
McCormick yelled back. "Say, where the hell does
this thing go, when and if we ever get there?" He
told us an artillery officer would be along the
road, waiting.
     I sat on top of the case and off we
started. Shells were dotting the fields in good
fashion as we arrived at the outpost, where we
were stopped by the M.P. "Absolutely no traveling
by car to Mandres. The whole area's under shell
fire, it stops and starts and "God knows when it's
gong to end," he said as he held up his hand.
McCormick told him we absolutely had to take our
chances on getting through; he explained we had a
case of shells on board, going to a battery in
urgent need of ammunition. The M.P. ran into the
dugout, and the officer in charge came out. After
a few minutes of talk he gave his O.K. for us to
proceed.
     He looked at me sitting on the case.
"Buddy, if I were you I'd walk up there." I told
him I thought I was just as safe there as
anywhere. I didn't care much. Not that I was
brave, because there were men much braver than I
up there in the trenches, at the machine guns, and
at the artillery posts; those men lived with it
day and night.
     To see that artillery officer caked with
mud, asleep on his feet -- what a hellish night he

must have had! -- made my job seem very small
indeed.

It was a lonesome and tortuous trip from
the outpost to Mandres. We passed two Mosquito
ambulances on the way back with the wounded;
outside of that there wasn't a human to be seen.
Only the noise of exploding shells. When we
arrived at the entrance to Mandres an artillery
officer with four or five soldiers were standing
along the road. As they spotted the iron case they
ran to greet us, and it wasn't long before they
were carting it across the field to a dugout about
three hundred feet off the road.

We immediately went to the church, now
being used as a morgue, where about a hundred and
fifty men were lying in rows, taking up every inch
of space. The Germans had made a horrible mess of
some. The picture is just as vivid today as it was
that April morning twenty-two years ago when I
entered the battered portals of that ruined
village church. It will stay with me, I suppose,
until my brain withers and passes on.

The rough floor was covered with the dew of
battle -- blood. Silently I walked between the
rows of still men. It was a terrible sight. Bodies
with arms and legs that hung to the forms only in
shreds, and faces that were nothing but a mass of
mangled pulp. I was walking along with Lieutenant
McCormick when I noticed a fine leather jacket
lined with sheepskin on top of an infantry
officer. I turned to McCormick and said, "That's a
fine-looking jacket." I stooped and picked it up
to examine it, and what a sight it uncovered!

His entire stomach and chest was blown
away. Someone had thrown the jacket over him to
hide the gruesome sight.

I could feel myself sway. Beads of
perspiration started to rise on my forehead. I hit
for the open; my stomach churned and growled. I
had never been sicker. As I was bending over,
losing my breakfast, a tap on the shoulder brought
me to my senses. "What's the trouble, Buddy?" I

looked around. Standing before me was a Sergeant
of Infantry; his arm was bandaged and carried in a
sling. Fresh blood was still oozing from the
wound, he was covered with mud, and blood-stains
spotted his uniform. I explained to him that I had
just seen something that didn't agree with my
breakfast. He asked me if this was my first trip
to the front. I told him I had been up many times
before; I asked him if he had been inside. "No, I
haven't," he said slowly. "I'm afraid to go in.
Some of my buddies are in there, I know."
    He told me it had been a wicked night. The
Germans started with a heavy barrage and in the
early morning hundreds of them swooped down on our
trenches in a surprise hand grenade attack. He
said it was terrible; the men were caught like
rats in a trap. Grenades were thrown right into
the trenches and there was no possible means of
escape. I asked him his trouble. He said he had
gotten off lucky, he went over on a counter attack
and coming back received a small piece of shrapnel
in his arm. He had been to the first aid station
and was waiting for transportation to the hospital
in the rear, to have it removed. He also told me
they were still bringing in the dead from the
trenches. I sat down on the old broken stone step
of the church to settle myself for a few minutes.
A shell would crash every now and then in the
ruins of the village and send white clouds of dust
and stone into the air.
    I entered the church again, where the rest
of the group was busy, trying to identify the
bodies. Some of the dog tags had been shot away,
others had been mangled so, they could not be
identified, and they were going through their
pockets in hopes of finding a letter or something
that would give their names. It was a mean job.
    All the space in the French Cemetery had
been used, and I was ordered by Lieut. McCormick
to plot a piece of ground running parallel to the
rear wall of the existing cemetery, which was
directly in back of the church. I went out and was

soon busy with tape lines and stakes, plotting the
first American cemetery in France directly on the
lines.

The plot on the north, facing the trenches,
was bounded by a row of light field guns in
dugouts. Most of the time I was out there they
were throwing a barrage into the enemy lines. I
could hear the German shells whistling through the
air, going on to the rear of our position. I had
been out there about a half hour when suddenly I
heard a dull thud. The ground vibrated and then
the explosion. A shell landed at the far corner of
the cemetery, hitting the stone wall and sending
pieces of stone flying through the air. I dropped
to the ground and stayed there for a few minutes.
Finally I got up and walked down to see the
damage.

The shell must have been of light caliber,
because it only took about two feet of the wall
away and the dent in the ground was just about
three feet in diameter.

It took me about an hour and a half to
finish the job, and I had almost finished when an
officer appeared from one of the artillery
dugouts. He walked over and wanted to know what I
was doing out there with a bunch of string and a
tape in my hand. I explained I was plotting out a
cemetery. "You'd better get the hell into this
dugout or somebody will be planting you in a
cemetery." He also warned me about gas shells that
were dropping about half a mile to the east of us.
I told him I had been there quite a while and that
I was just about finished. "All right, soldier,"
he answered, and down he went into the dugout
again. In the afternoon things had quieted down
considerably. A detail was sent to dig the long
line of trenches. Records were completed. The men
were wrapped in burlap and gently laid side by
side. An officer read the burial services. The
slow, melancholy notes of taps floated through the
breeze. That was the end of the first boys of the
gallant Yankee Division to make the supreme

sacrifice. The most violent attack so far launched
against the American forces was now history. That
was one day I was glad to get away from Mandres.
Not many words passed between us on our way down
the road; we were all occupied with our own
thoughts.

Nancy

In the evening McCormick and the group jumped into the little truck and paid a visit to Nancy. Nancy is about twenty miles east of Toul and considerably larger than Toul. Trolleys run on the streets, and it is typical of the middle class cities you might see here at home. It has an immense park with winding walks. Big trees with wide branches throw an abundance of shade over spots set aside for the children to play. Little fountains banked by shrubs and flowers dot the landscape.

The birds chirp and jump from limb to limb and people feed the little squirrels just the same as they do here in our own parks. I always enjoyed a few minutes here, just sitting on a bench watching the youngsters romp and play. I didn't have to stretch my imagination very far to picture myself somewhere in Fairmont park.

Off from the center of town a block or two was Place-de-Stanislaus, where the public buildings were located. You entered a large paved court through immense iron gates. They were hand wrought and seemed to be very old. The detail was very delicate and well studied, and the bars swept in graceful curves, forming the most beautiful symmetry of design, which the French know how to handle so well.

Flanking the court were the buildings, designed in the French Renaissance. In the immense auditorium of one of these buildings we listened to a French orchestra give a concert on the Forth of July, in honor of the American soldiers. The Cafe Lorraine, as I remember, was the leading social center. I enjoyed a couple of really delicious meals there. They served a bottle of

wine with the meal, as is the custom in France.
The French people drink very little water; in fact
they never serve us water with our meal unless we
request it.

Another thing I enjoyed was going through
the big market place. The dressed meats with
little bunches of parsley tucked neatly around
them certainly looked appetizing, and the fresh
vegetables, brought in by the peasant farmers in
their picturesque two-wheel carts, often drawn by
a team of oxen, smelled so fresh and sweet. You
know how I love watermelon. One day, going through
the market, I noticed a melon. It looked just like
ours, except that it was perfectly round. I asked
the little chubby women standing at the stall if
it was a watermelon. "Oui, oui, Monsieur." "A real
American watermelon?" I insisted. "Oui, oui
Monsieur." Well, I bought it, and could hardly
wait till I got it to the tent.

With four of five of the boys standing
around and teeth floating in my mouth, I sliced it
down the middle, and what a disappointment! It may
have been a French watermelon, but it certainly
didn't have any of the characteristics of our good
red American melon. I was so mad I wouldn't touch
a bit of it, and the fellows finished it up and
nailed a piece of rind on the center pole of the
tent, so I could at least be reminded of what the
outside of a real American watermelon looked like.

One thing I found early in army life; it
did no good to get sore about anything. You got
very little sympathy and there was always somebody
on hand to needle you, or a practical joker to
work on you, if one took himself too seriously or
went off balance. A buck private in Uncle Sam's
Army is a buck private to every other buck. It
makes no difference whether he is worth a month's
pay or many times that, he's just another buck,
and rightly so. That is the esprit-de-corps that
has made Uncle Sam's army the finest in the world.

Commendation from
General Pershing

One afternoon about a month after the
bloody baptismal encounter of the Yankee Division
at Seicheprey, Lieut. McCormick called the group
together. While we stood at attention, and the
Stars and Stripes floated in the gentle breeze at
his side, he read the following that had just
arrived by courier from Chaumont, General
Pershing's headquarters.

AMERICAN EXPEDITIONARY FORCES
HEADQUARTERS SERVICES OF SUPPLY
OFFICE OF THE CHIEF QUARTERMASTER, A.E.F.
GRAVES REGISTRATION SERVICE

G.R.S   :
Bulletin: *France, May 19, 1918*
No. 1   :

        The following letter of commendation is
published for the information of the G.R.S. and
in recognition of courage and efficiency in which
the Chief of this Service has taken great pride:

GENERAL HEADQUARTERS
AMERICAN EXPEDITIONARY FORCES
Off:14790-a-50-PF   France, May 15, 1918.

From: The Commander in Chief.

To: The Chief Quartermaster, A.E.F., Hq. S.O.S.

Subject: Commendation

1. I have heard with great pleasure of the excellent work and fine conduct of the members of Headquarters Advance Group No. 1, Graves Registration Service, who are mentioned herein. The work preformed by these men under heavy shell fire and gas on April 20th, 1918, and the days immediately succeeding, at Mandres and vicinity, is best described herin:

"On April 20th, Lieut. McCormick and his group arrived at Mandres and began their work under heavy shell fire and gas, and although troops were in dugouts, these men went immediately to the cemetery, and in order to preserve records and locations repaired and erected new crosses as fast as the old ones were blown down. They also completed the extension to the cemetery, this work occupying a period of one and a half hours, during which time, shells were falling continually, and they were subjected to mustard gas. They gathered many bodies which had been first in the hands of the Germans, and were later retaken by American counter-attacks. Identification was especially difficult, all papers and tags having been removed, and most of the bodies being in a terrible condition and beyond recognition. The Lieutenant in command particularly mentions Sergeant Keating and Privates La Rue and Murphy, as having been responsible for the most gruesome part of the work of identification, examining every body most thoroughly, searching for scars or tattoo marks and where bodies were blown to pieces, these men were especially careful to make minute examination, regardless of the danger attendant upon their work. This group of men was in charge of everything at Mandres from the time the bodies were brought in, until they were interned and marked with crosses and proper name plates were attached."
2. The splendid work and conduct of

2nd Lieut. Homer B. McCormick, Inf. U.S.R.Q.M.C
Commanding Advance Goup No. 1, G.R.S

Quartermaster Sergt. Sr. Grade, Charles P. Keating
Unit 301, G.R.S

Private Holmes E. La Rue Jr., Unit 301, G.R.S

Private Raymond A. Murphy, Unit 301 G.R.S

during this trying period is appreciated by all
throughout the command.

By direction: *J.W. McAndrew*
Chief of Staff"

After he dismissed the group, the
Lieutenant called me over to one side and told me
he could not understand why my name had not been
mentioned in the commendation.

"Don't let it trouble you, " I replied "If
I get home alive that will be enough commendation
for me."

In fact, my end of it was painted a little
to flowery at that. It was warm up there, but not
quite so warm as pictured. The boys working in the
battle-scarred church did have a gruesome job. I
needed the open air. After all, there was nothing
so important about my job. Plotting cemeteries was
not so spectacular. It was a mean, depressing
assignment, but that was the part I was to play in
the Service. Nevertheless, I was proud of the fact
that in the line of duty I was called upon to plot
the first American cemetery at the front. At times
I got at least within hailing distance of the real
men in the trenches and it made me feel that,
small as my job was, I together with the rest of
my group had arrived at the most advanced position
on the lines called for in the duty of our
service. With all this our experiences were tamed
compared to the doughboys who pushed forward at

Cantigny, Belleau Wood, Chateau Thierry and the
Argonne.
        Some days later, McCormick called the group
to attention again and read them a bulletin. You
will find it tucked away with my original
documents.

Elsie Janis

One bright sunny afternoon in mid-spring, several of the boys were sitting on a bench outside our tent. General Edwards strolled by, accompanied by two women. We jumped to attention. The General smiled and waved for us to be seated. One woman in smart uniform with a service cap cocked at a jaunty angle, smiled and waved her hand. "Sunning yourselves, boys?" It was the sweetheart of the A.E.F. All the boys loved her, and this country can never repay her for the good she did in France during those dark days. The other woman, as you may guess, her constant companion, was Mother Janis, a beautiful character, carrying a smile as big as Elsie's.

I never missed one of her concerts if it was possible to get there. One late afternoon we walked to Menil-la-Tour to hear her. She was standing in the boxing ring off the main road. Father Conner, a chaplain of the 26th Division, had this erected, and arranged bouts for the boys. He was a fine man and did a lot to lift the morale and spirit of the troops. A soldier was seated at the piano, and a great crowd of soldiers were banked on all sides. Miss Janis was having a grand time kidding the boys with her little impromptu sayings. Soon the piano started, and she began her army ditties, - "Beautiful Ka-Katy," "Over There, " "Mademoiselle from Bar-le-Duc," "There's a Long, Long Trail" -- as no one else could sing them.

All the time she was singing, big army trucks were rolling along, going north with supplies. Elsie tried to compete with the trucks, but finally she stopped. "Hey!" she shouted, spreading her legs apart and hands planted on her hips in characteristic fashion. "If General

Edwards don't hold up this war for fifteen
minutes, I'm licked." I don't know whether the
General was in the audience, but all traffic was
stopped and Elsie finished her song fest and the
crowd milled around her, and she had a tough time
getting away.

Menil-la-Tour, the scene of our baptism in
this part of the war-torn country, was not much to
look at. It was the typical French hamlet type,
but it seemed to be the focal point of the Toul
Sector, situated about midway between Toul and the
front lines. It had been the First Division
headquarters and now the 26th.

I remember one morning we were in the
village. Everything seemed tense, and there was an
air of excitement about. Army cars were parked all
around and there seemed to be an abundance of
officers. Movie camera men and photographers were
perched on the terrace wall of the Headquarters
Building. We asked what was going on, and found
that Secretary of War Baker was expected shortly.
He arrived; camera men started their shots,
officers ran out of the door to shake hands with
him. He turned and waved to the small group of
soldiers watching from the road, and then went
inside. I got a funny feeling as I looked at him.
"By gosh, he's lucky! He can go home whenever he
wants." I have often wondered whether that thought
struck any of the other boys that way.

The Death of
Major Lufberry

The bells in the tower of the great Gothic
Cathedral at Toul were calling the faithful to
Mass. The air was crisp and the gentle breezes of
late spring carried sweet fragrance of new life in
the budding. It was a beautiful Sunday morning;
the sky was a deep blue -- not a cloud floated in
the heavens. We had just returned from Mass in the
little village near by. Everything seemed so
peaceful, even the guns along the front were
silent, sensing, it seemed, the mockery of
disturbing the tranquility of this beautiful
Sabbath morning. But War, the star of this age,
would not be cast aside for long, jealous lest the
people forget him momentarily to look at the
wonders of nature God had given them. Soon the
silence was broken. Anti-aircraft guns atop the
hill at Toul began to bark. The blue sky soon
became dotted with little balls of smoke as the
shells exploded in the air. We scanned the sky to
find the invader, but he was traveling so high it
was difficult to spot him at first. Finally we
caught a glimpse of him as his plane swung in
different angles against the sun. At times when
the sun hit him broadside he would glisten like a
silver bird and then quickly pass out of sight
again.

Suddenly we heard the roar of a motor; a
plane was leaving the field of the 94th Squadron,
directly to the east of us. He started in the
direction of the lines, and some few minutes later
came back over the field again, but this time very
high. He continued circling over the field,
gaining altitude until we almost lost sight of

him. About ten minutes later the tat-tat-tat of the machine guns told us the start of a battle that was to mean death to a gallant American ace of the air was on. They circled in wide loops; you would see one plane coming in sight as it swept toward the earth, then the tat-tat as the other plane swept down behind it, then a turn; the first plane with a graceful swing would turn and sweep into the heavens again. This maneuvering for position kept on and on, until finally they disappeared beyond the horizon in the direction of Nancy. Lost from view, we could still hear the sound of the guns as they fought it out high in the heavens on that beautiful morning. Finally everything seemed peaceful again. The faint echo of combat had faded away, the sky was clear again and the smoke of battle had mingled with the deep blue above us. I went over to the bench in front of my tent and sat down. I was by myself. I was not sentimental, because by this time I had become hardened to the life Fate had chosen me to be a part of. I had seen a little, had been through the baptism of fire. I was in a sense a veteran in the business of war, and yet I wondered at the mystery of it all. What it was all about? Why men were born and privileged to live for moments only in such a beautiful universe, where the sun cast its golden glow upon the fields, the forests and the streams by day, and millions of diamonds studded the heavens in the darkness of night? -- had to turned their land into a living hell, where the soil of the fields blotted the soaking blood of their brothers and where men sent other men dropping in flaming spirals from the sky.

About noon, word reached us that the battle of the air was over. The man we saw leave the field a few hours before would never land again. A bullet found its mark; the plane burst into flames and fell, midway between Toul and Nancy. The pilot jumped from the flaming inferno and crashed to earth a hundred feet away from a small stream. A great hush came over the hospital ground as the

charred and broken body of the American ace
entered the gates.

"Slats" Murphy, a member of our group,
embalmed the body, and Captain Eddie Rickenbacker,
I believe, brought over his dress uniform. I
happened to drop over to the little room when they
were putting his uniform on. His legs to the hips
were badly burned, but fortunately his face was in
good condition. His closely cropped mustache and
eyebrows were singed slightly and one hand had a
machine gun bullet wound.

He was laid out in state in one of the
large rooms on the Hospital grounds. Flowers were
banked thick around the coffin. High ranking
officials, civil and military, of all the Allied
Nations marched behind the flag-draped casket, as
it slowly crept along the winding lane toward the
little cemetery nestled in the orchard. Hundreds
of planes swooped low with motors wide open,
dropping big bouquets of flowers all along the
march. It was a beautiful and impressive sight.
The road was strewn with flowers, some dropping on
the casket and breaking, spreading tiny petals
like flakes of snow. All during the burial service
bouquets dropped form the heavens until the drab,
cold field looked like a rose garden in full
bloom. A deserving tribute to a gallant ace!
Before leaving, I picked up a few flowers and
sent them home to Nanna. She still has them, dried
and withered, pressed between the leaves of her
favorite book.

The German aviator who brought Lufberry
down never reached home. He was sent hurtling to
his death just as he was about to cross the lines.
So two men who lived on that glorious Sabbath morn
were to be no more, as the sun, in a brilliant
ball of fire, sank beneath the western hills to
end the day - their day!

Many a time during those spring and summer
days I watched the sun set beyond the horizon and
wondered what the coming day would bring.

Summer 1918

Spring had faded and the long days of
summer were upon us. More American divisions were
going into the line that was now extending from
the Nancy sector in the east almost to Verdun on
the west. The French had gradually been relieved
of this sector to strengthen the forces fighting
the drive on Paris. This was a terrific onslaught.
The Germans were breaking through the defense and
creating a great bulge in the line, touching
within forty miles of Paris. Things looked
critical for a time in the spring and early
summer. American divisions, including the U.S.
Marines, were rushed into the lines, and met the
Germans. A bloody battle started. The Germans
inflicted heavy casualties on our boys, but the
resistance held. A wedge was driven into the great
bulge by our troops, and the German offensive was
checked. This was the last great drive attempted
by the Germans. Plans were now in the making for
three major drives by the Allied forces. The
French and English to drive along the Western
Front in the direction of the German-Belgian
border, the American forces in the center driving
through the Argonne in the direction of Sedan, and
also in the east through St. Mihiel in the
direction of Metz.

With the extension of our lines westward we
were kept busy trying to cover the additional
ground. We visited many French cemeteries and
little patches of graves just behind the lines,
getting records and erecting crosses over the
graves. I remember one afternoon we took a trip to
a little village cemetery across from Mont Sec. A
soldier who was familiar with the graves was

showing me around. The cemetery was enclosed with
a stone wall about seven feet high; there was an
opening about six feet wide, with iron gates, in
the center of the two walls. The one in the
direction of Mont Sec we opened, and walked out in
the open to check on a few scattered graves.
Presently I heard a dull thud against the wall
back of us. The fellow with me yelled, "Drop flat
on your belly!" Down I went as fast as I could.
"Sounds as if somebody's throwing stones around
here." "Throwing stones, hell," he said, "there
are snipers over on the hill, taking pot shots at
us." We crawled along on our bellies in the high
weeds to the gate, and got within the shelter of
the wall again. I took no more chances checking
those graves that day.

Summer nights spend under canvas at
Sebastopol were not bad; except for rainy weather
we kept the side flaps open, and it was very
healthy and invigorating. Of course we were
disturbed many times by night raiders trying to
bomb the air drome to the east of us. One night
they were especially annoying. It was pitch dark,
and they kept circling overhead for hours,
dropping flares to get position. There was no use
trying to sleep, so we stood outside the tent,
with our helmets on to protect ourselves from the
fragments of steel falling from the exploding
anti-aircraft shells. Already they had dropped a
number around the air drome.

Doosey and I were talking, when suddenly a
hissing sound came through the air. The bomb land;
it shook the ground like an earthquake and pieces
of hot molten steel flew high into the air. I was
in my stocking feet; my legs started and off I
went on a run as fast as I could across the road.
It had just been resurfaced with broken stone, and
the sharp edges certainly chewed my feet in good
fashion. I stopped as quickly as I had started.
When I came back, Bill laughed, "Fine brave
soldier you are." Well, to this day I don't know
what started my legs in motion so fast, nor can I

tell what stopped them so suddenly; just one of
those things you can't explain, I guess. The next
morning we walked over to see the crater about 450
feet from the tent; it was some twelve feet in
diameter and about six feet deep -- big enough
almost to put our tent in.

Now that the weather was warm, many
patients were out doors, some hobbling along on
crutches, others in wheel chairs. Archie
Roosevelt, son of Theodore Roosevelt, one of our
great Presidents, was at the hospital for some
time. He had been badly shot up in an engagement
on the front lines. We saw him frequently, walking
around the grounds, trying to regain his strength.
One day on my way to the hospital cemetery I met
his brother, Theodore Jr., hiking it up the road
to see his brother. He looked every inch a
soldier, with the Traditional dirt of the front
lines.

My First Leave

Late in the summer I got my first leave, to
stay away overnight. Three or four of us,
including your Uncle Jim, left for Toul, Saturday
afternoon, and did not have to report back until
Sunday night. We arrived in Toul with a real
holiday spirit. We headed right for the cafe and
restaurant where we usually stopped when in town,
and enjoyed a big steak dinner, French fried
potatoes, sliced tomatoes with French dressing,
cucumbers smothered with onions, peas with milk
dressing, a cup of hot chocolate and topped off
with a French pastry. After the meal we began to
worry about getting rooms, which was a new problem
to us. We asked the mademoiselle that had served
us if she knew where we could get rooms for the
night. She informed us that Madame had very nice
rooms. Fine. We decided to stay there.

We all went up to look our rooms over. Your
Uncle Jim and I had a room in the rear,
overlooking the back garden. Vines crept along the
garden wall, little bird-houses on bark poles
stood here and there, and a bird bath stood
majestically in the center of a flagstone circle.
A little wooden gate with turned spindles and hung
by wrought iron strap hinges opened to a grove of
trees beyond. The room was carpeted with heavy
broadloom that seemed to sink ankle-deep when you
walked. Venetian blinds were at the windows, with
pull curtains of light blue. The four-poster bed
was heavily carved and covered with a lace canopy
and a feather mattress that must have been
eighteen inches thick. From the ceiling hung a
glass chandelier that could have graced the
ballroom of any of our finest hotels. And last,
but not least, an honest-to-goodness toilet --

something I hadn't sat on for many, many months.
As far as I was concerned I was ready to sit in
the big easy chair near the window, take off my
shoes, call for a dozen magazines and stay there
till it was time to go back to war. All Uncle Jim
did was to walk around the bed, punching the
mattress to see how deep his hand would sink in.
It was the first time we had seen a bedroom in
nine or ten months, and believe me, it looked
pretty good.

We went to the Cinema that night, but all
the way through the show I was itching to get back
to that room, just like a youngster wanting to get
back to his toys. After the show we stopped in the
Grill Room of our "hotel" and had a bottle of beer
before retiring. We jumped into bed, and it seemed
as if we were floating in mid air, but the
expected sleep of the blessed did not come so
fast. We both rolled and tossed, lying on one side
and then the other. Some time after we were in
bed, I asked Uncle Jim how he was making out. "I
don't know, I can't seem to get use to this damned
thing. If you'd keep over on your own side maybe I
could get to sleep." The mattress sloped toward
the center, and try as we would we couldn't help
getting tangled up with each other. Well, we just
cat-napped through the night, and every time I
turned over in a half-doze, I had the feeling I
was climbing up a mountain, with my hands trying
to grasp something lest I fall down. I guess that
was when I was deep in the center of the bed and
trying to pull myself to the side.

The next morning we asked the other fellows
how they slept. It was the same story. The sudden
transformation was to much for us. One of the
fellows dreamed he was in a manure pit, that he
was smothering to death, and the more he kicked
and squirmed the deeper he sank in the mire. When
he awoke in the morning the top sheet was on the
floor. And so passed our first night in a French
bed.

We had a grand time Sunday, doing exactly
what we wanted. Ham and eggs for breakfast, and
then to the ten o'clock Mass in the ancient
Cathedral of Toul with its towering spires that
could be seen for miles around. In the afternoon
we attended the band concert in the square near
the Y.M.C.A

The First German
Planes Downed

It was in this square that the first two
German planes to fall victims to American aviators
with Pershing's Army were on exhibition.

The fight occurred around nine o'clock on a
Sunday morning in early April. We were attracted
by the noise of the anti-aircraft gun on the hill
at Toul. We looked toward the sky and saw two tiny
specks over the town of Toul. Two planes left the
airdrome; one was piloted by Lieut. Alan Winslow
and the other by Lieut. "Doug" Campbell. The
German planes evidently saw them leave the field
for they started down to meet them at a terrific
burst of speed. It wasn't long before the fight
started. Wide loops, half turns, spirals and the
noise of the machine guns went on for some
minutes. We could see it all very plainly, as by
this time they were almost over the airdrome, only
a short distance away. Finally the plane piloted
by Winslow got directly on the tail of one German
plane and a maddening dash for the ground began.
He tried to zigzag and turn, but Winslow kept
right in back with his machine gun roaring all the
time. The bullet-riddled plane was forced to land
about a mile away from the landing field. How the
pilot escaped death with that hail of lead
surrounding him I don't know, but he climbed out
of the plane unscratched. In the meantime Campbell
and his Boche were still at it, while Winslow
circled to gain altitude and go into the fight to
help his comrade. He got above the German and was
just about to dive when the tracer bullets from
Campbell's gun found their mark. The plane burst
into flames and went crashing to the ground. The

two enemy planes crashed less than two minutes
apart.

It was a great Sunday afternoon in Toul;
the town was crowded with people and the farmers
from the adjacent villages who saw the battle came
to town to participate in the celebration.

A guard of honor was stationed around the
planes and a French military band played well into
the night.

Toul was a popular center for American
aviators. During their free time they would jump
into the car and come here to relax momentarily
from their grueling duties. I saw Luffberry,
Rickenbacker and many of the boys from the 94th on
numerous occasions. Eddie Rickenbacker was a
quiet, unassuming sort of fellow, usually trailing
along by himself, seeming to get a kick out of the
window shopping. Frequently we would take a run
over to the airdrome and watch the planes come in
from patrol duty. To look at some of them you
would wonder how they ever made the field.
Rickenbacker landed one day with the fabric on one
wing almost in shreds, and the body of the plane
sprayed with so many machine gun bullet holes made
me wonder how he ever came back. Theirs was a
messy business, so no one begrudged them the
little pleasure they picked up while off duty.

Back to War

Well, all good things must end. We had had
a fine weekend in Toul, and arrived back to
Sebastopol and our little tent around eight
o'clock Sunday evening. The mail man had arrived
and I found a packet of letters on my bunk. One
was from Yvonne of Goncourt. It was in answer to
one I sent her in the spring, telling her all
about our experiences at the Front. I had asked
her to pray for all the boys, and for the France
she loved so dearly, when she went to Mass on
Sundays in the little village chapel high on the
hill. Her letter, like herself, was plain and
childlike in expression, just a little over one
page long.

She wanted to send me the ring, "but the
post service is very bad in France." "You will
soon forget," she wrote, "petite Mademoiselle
Yvonne, when you promenade with the gay
mademoiselles on the Grand Boulevards."

It was a welcomed letter, but all over so
fast. I could have listened to so much more.

The trip to Toul must have spoiled me
somewhat. The following day I turned my nose up at
the mess. I got hungry later on, so I bought a can
of jam and a loaf of French bread. After my fill,
I put the can under my bunk and covered it with a
piece of canvas to protect it from the golden-
backed bees that buzzed thickly around the tent
during the day.

One afternoon shortly after, Tillie La Rue
called for me to look in the tent. There was Tyson
sound asleep, flat on his back, with his arms up
and the back of his hand resting in the palms of
his hands. He looked so peaceful. Now if there was

anything Ty hated it was to be disturbed while he
was enjoying one of these midsummer siestas.

La Rue said, "If we could only do something
to break this up." Right away I though of the jam
and the bees. I let La Rue in on the secret.
"Fine," he said. "You get the jam and I'll gather
the gang." A joke was no good unless an audience
was on hand to enjoy it. So I got the can, opened
the lid wide, took some jam and rubbed it all over
the outside of the can and put it under Ty's bunk.
The gang was all around the tent looking in under
the flaps.

Pretty soon the bees began to work. They
swarmed under the bunk and over it. Presently they
started to get acquainted. Ty was a sound sleeper,
but the confusion of the enemy made him stir a
little. Finally one more bold than the rest gently
touched his cheek and was off again. Ty took one
arm and swished across his face, then he let his
hand fall to the side of the bunk. It wasn't long
now before half a dozen were crawling over his
hand. Ty's hand came up like a shot, his eyes
opened and his feet went up into the air. For a
minute he could not get his bearings, his arms and
legs went in all directions, trying to chase his
little playmates. Finally the gang had to let
loose. With that, Ty knew something was in the
wind, and he started to investigate. He looked
under his bunk and found the can of jam. He tilted
the bunk a little, gave the can a terrific kick
that sent it flying out of the tent, then he
turned to the gang, clenched his fist and said, "I
could lick the . . . . . . that did that." As he
was about eight inches taller than your dad, I
didn't take up the challenge.

Joe Anisman became acquainted with a Jewish
family in Toul and they invited him down to supper
about once a week. Upon his return, about eleven
o'clock, he would visit every bunk and shake the
fellows until they were wide awake, and then say,
"Madame Merish of Toul bonjour Messieurs." This
used to get Caswell, our staid New Englander's,

goat. He would roll over, give a disgusted grunt and pull the blankets over his head. One night he got so mad he threw a shoe at Joe, but it missed its mark and went right through the stove pipe and knocked it down. It was up to Joe to put it together, and we had a lot of fun lying on our bunks watching him fussing with it. By the time he finished putting it together, he looked like one of our stevedore friends from the South.

Doosey was the best natured fellow I ever met; nothing seemed to bother him, his face always carried a big grin. "What the hell are you guys gripin' about?" he said one day when we were feeling pretty low. "Why, you never had it so good in all your lives. You get your clothes for nothin', your eats for nothin', they blow a horn to tell you when to get up, they blow it to tell you when to eat, and even blow it to tell you when to go to sleep. And then they top it off at the end of every month by payin' you for labor well done lyin' flat on your back, keepin' your fanny warm, just like I'm doing now!"

Trip Along the Lines

One afternoon late in the summer, McCormick sent for me to come to his office. A big Italian make car was standing outside with a soldier at the wheel. I went inside and McCormick introduced me to a Captain Stanley Muckleston of the U.S. Marine Corps. He was a snappy looking officer, about 26 years old.

McCormick explained that Mcukleston was connected with our service and wanted some one with experience to take a three or four day trip along the lines with him, in order to make a survey of possible cemetery sites. Plans were rapidly crystallizing now for the two great drives of the American Forces through the Argonne Forest and St. Mihiel. By this time we had over a million men in France and thousands more landing daily at the ports of England and France. Our own little service that arrived in November of 1917 with fifty men now numbered well over a thousand.

I returned to the tent to get my few little necessities. McCormick loaned me a small canvas traveling bag, and with that thrown over my shoulder I was all set. Captain Muckleston was in the back seat and I started to jump in with the chauffeur. Muckleston beckoned for me to come sit with him. That was the beginning of a happy and warm friendship that lasted until the spring of 1919, when I rode with him to the station at Neufchateau to board a train for a base port on his way to the States -- a sick youngster and broken in spirit. I never saw or heard from him again. I have often wondered where he is and what he is doing now. Just like I wonder about hundreds of other fellows it had been my privilege to meet during those long twenty months in France.

We had an extensive trip and covered may miles along the lines, where our troops were in action. One night we were invited to spend the night in a monastery high on the hill, buried in the seclusion of a deep forest. When I returned from this trip I set down on my bunk and in the candle glow I sent Nanna and Grand-Dad a letter, telling them about it. Here it is -- I think it will tell you better than I can remember.

Somewhere in France
August 23, 1918

Dear Parents:
I took a very interesting trip the other day with a Captain Muckleston of the Marines, to make a survey of possible cemetery sites. We rode in a big Italian car driven by a chauffeur. I felt like a Captain myself instead of a mere buck private.
We stopped over night in a little village not far from a city we all heard about some two years ago, made famous by the great battle fought there -- Verdun.
We arrived here about 9 p.m. and were met by a French Captain who took us to an old monastery on the outskirts of the village, built hundreds of years ago, situated high on the hill in a forest of trees.
We entered a large room, lined with heavy oak paneling and carving of the most delicate detail. It was furnished very plain; the threadbare carpet looked as if it had been there for ages and the furniture had lost its lustre long ago.
Flickering candles in highly ornamented silver candlesticks cast faint dreamy rays around the room. A huge oil painting of the Crucifixion centered between two large casement windows, draped in cardinal red curtains.

*In one corner of the room was a big
shepherd dog playing with a small kitten. In the
center of the room, at a big oak desk, sat an old
monk reading a prayer book. He wore a cassock and
girdle.*

*The candle at his side cast a soft glow on
the snow white locks that fell deep over his
forehead.*

*As we approached he closed his prayer-book;
rising, he greeted us with a deep bow, then
clasping his hands together, said in excellent
English, "Ah, Americans."*

*The officer spoke in French, asking
permission to spend the night there. The monk
gravely bowed in acquiescence.*

*He took one of the large silver
candlesticks with the flickering light and led us
to the hall and up a great winding stair to the
third floor, and showed us to our rooms, or cells,
as they call them. They were about seven feet wide
and ten feet long, furnished with nothing more
than a cot, small table and chair with a small
crucifix hanging on the white washed wall at the
head of the cot.*

*We then returned to the big room and the
monk went to a small cupboard and returned with a
large silver container and small red glasses on a
tray. He filled our glasses with a delicious
smooth wine that just hit the spot. He informed us
that it came from old casks that have been used
for over three hundred years.*

*We sipped and chatted for a half hour or
so, and then, each holding a candle, trod our way
up the creaking stairs to our rooms.*

*In the silence of my room I could hear the
heavy guns booming in the distance. I looked out
the window. It was a beautiful night, the moon was
full and it cast deep speckled shadows along the
ground as it peered through the thick foliage of
the forest.*

*I spent a peaceful night in the old world,
and the next morning, bright and early, we were*

on our way. This is a fascinating life over here -
- you never know what the next day may bring. We
spend a night in the peaceful atmosphere of a
monastery, and the next night -- well, you just
don't know. Our trip lasted three days. We covered
a lot of ground and were kept quite busy making
notes for our report, which is to be forwarded to
General Headquarters.

Yesterday I had quite a different trip.
Lieut. McCormick and I went up to the third line
Trenches -- Seicheprey - to try and locate two
boys who are buried up there, but the ground is so
Churned from artillery fire I doubt if we ever
will find them.

McCormick had his field glasses. We could
see the German trenches and miles of barbed wire
zigzagging in all directions over No Man's Land.
We had a good view of Mont Sec, which towers high
above the flat plains. We also saw a very exciting
air battle; it lasted for some fifteen minutes,
but evidently ended in a draw, as the combatants
separated and went in different directions.

Well, dear parents, I must close, as it is
very late. Rain drops are hitting fast on the
Canvas above me. Fritz won't worry us tonight, so
I will enjoy the sleep of the blessed, -- the
first in three weeks, outside of my peaceful
slumber in the monastery. I wish all nights could
be like that.

Your loving son,
John

A few weeks after my trip with Muckleston,
I received a little certificate from Uncle Sam. I
was now a sergeant. Your Uncle Jim was already a
sergeant. Together with his other duties he took
care of all the office work connected with the
group, which had been enlarged somewhat, and was
doing a fine job.

St Mihiel

The St. Mihiel salient had been the scene of bitter fighting in the early years of the war. The Crown Prince of Germany drove his armies on the West to Verdun and on the East an army drove down the valley from Metz.

By holding the salient it enabled the Germans to control the Commercy-Verdun railway running to Toul and Nancy, thus cutting communication with Verdun from the Meuse Valley and the east.

In 1915-1916 the French made desperate drives to recapture St. Mihiel, but were repulsed with heavy losses.

Two or three days after the advance of St. Mihiel's drive, we visited this historical city. It had been damaged very little, although the Germans held it since 1914.

Most of the fighting had occurred to the west of it in the direction of Verdun and to the east in the direction of Pont-a-Mousson. While here we visited the public buildings designed in early Renaissance, and the Church of St. Etienne, where fortunately the great work of Ligier Richier, the noted sculptor of the sixteenth century and the French Renaissance period, were still intact. Richier, whose work can be seen in all the great cathedrals of France, built during that period, was a native son of St. Mihiel.

The First American Army

In June Pershing was anxious to establish
his own army, but the desperate state of the
Allies in the spring and mid-summer compelled him
to disperse his divisions among the French and
British armies. First to hold the great German
offensive, and then to turn back the enemy with
the brilliant actions of the First Division at
Cantigny, the Second Division and the Sixth
Marines at Belleau Wood and the Third Division at
the Chateau Thierry.

By late July the second battle of the Marne
was won. A general advance started in the
direction of the German border. Scattered American
divisions were now to be concentrated and the
first American operations were planned against the
St. Mihiel Salient. By August the American First
Army under General Persing's personal command was
organized.

Late August and early September was the
scene of great activity along the Toul Sector.
Every night under cover of darkness thousands of
troops with artillery marched along the roads and
settled in the surrounding villages close to the
lines.

The staff at the hospital had been
increased, additional cots were being installed in
the various buildings. The floors of the wooden
barracks were covered with straw.

It was apparent the drive through St.
Mihiel was close at hand. A half million troops
were concentrated in this area and yet everything
looked quite normal during the day. We visited the
lines the day before the drive. Everything seemed
quiet. We noticed new gun positions just off the
road that had been established under cover of

darkness, but they were cleverly camouflaged from
the air.

On the morning of the attack the line ran
westward from the Moselle Hills north of Pont-a-
Mousson hills straight out across the open Woevre
plains until it reached the foot of the Meuse
Hills at Apremont. Here it turned south and
touched the Meuse River just south of the old
French fort, Camp des Romains. Beyond the fort the
lines extended north, crossed the river in front,
of St. Mihiel.

It was not possible to attack the salient
from the west near St. Mihiel, owing to the
strength of the position on which Fort Camp des
Romains stands. From this point the view up and
down the valley was one of the most commanding on
the whole battle front.

On the east side of the Meuse Hills the
German had two important points from which his
view was almost as good as from Fort Camp des
Romains. One of his commanding sweeps was from the
Heights of Hattonchatel which surveyed the entire
Woevre plain. The other was from Mont Sec, one of
the most heavily fortified elevations on the
entire St. Mihiel front.

Mont Sec, a detached mound rising out of
the Woevre plains, was about a half mile inside
the German lines. It was a splendid piece of
military engineering. The ruined village of Mont
Sec at its base was turned into a series of
winding concrete pill boxes. Covered sidewalks led
back to a number of reinforced concrete caves cut
into the side of the hill to provide shelter for
the infantry.

Beyond these, cement steps and runways led
to a great open space driven into the middle of
the mound. From this rotunda, stairs led up to a
number of observation posts from which the Germans
could survey the surrounding country for miles.

The St. Mihiel Drive

On the night of September 11th, the First Army was in place. Four divisions, the 2nd, 5th, 82nd, and 90th, made up the First Corps under command of General Liggett. The Second Corps, under the command of General Dickmam, consisted of the 1st, 42nd and 89th Divisions.

They covered the line from Pont-a-Mousson to St. Mihiel. On the corner of St. Mihiel, driving east in the direction of Thiaucourt, was the 26th Yankee division, with the 15th French Colonial and the 4th American in reserve. Three more divisions were in reserve behind the Seicheprey, Mont Sec and Xirway lines. The total Americans and French numbered about 500,000 men, of which 60,000 were French. It was the greatest American army that had yet been assembled to go into battle.

I will never forget that September night. The sun dropped beyond the horizon in a brilliant red to end the day. The early evening was serene; a gentle breeze blew in from the west and a slight chilliness told us the summer was passing away. With the coming of night stars poked their twinkling lights through the darkness of the heavens. But with all the beauty of a September night the march of feet continued; the monotonous rattle of iron rimmed wheels grinding on the hard surface of the roads rolled over the quiet country side.

Around 11 o'clock the silence of the night was broken. Spasmodic flashes lit the sky to the north of us, as the guns sunken in the depths of the earth and under cover of leaves and twigs of trees began to send shells loaded with jagged pieces of steel through the air.

It was the beginning of a great battle. Men
under a sky studded with diamonds pushing heavy
cylinders of iron into long casings that pointed
to the sky. A sharp command, a thunderous roar
that shook the earth, a vicious snort of flame as
the demon of destruction started its travel
through the air to churn the earth and spread hot
particles of steel, many miles away.

Youngsters sitting in trenches, holding
rifles loaded with pencils of sharp pointed steel
and fixed bayonets of tempered steel ground to the
fineness of razor blade, waiting for the command
that would send them across a land that rose and
fell like the surface of the mid-Atlantic during a
great storm, and where miles of barbed wire wove
its way across the fields like a giant spider web.

Yes, many youngsters were sitting and
waiting for the zero hour that night, wondering
what the dawn would bring. I wonder many times
whether, if the thoughts that swept through the
trenches that night could be blazed before the
masses that make up this universe, ruthless
leaders would not find it more difficult to lead
their people on to slaughter.

A terrific barrage swept the entire front
from Pont-a-Mousson to St. Mihiel and kept on with
increased intensity until daylight. There was very
little sleep that night. Waves of English bombing
planes traveled back and forth all night, flares
lit the distant horizon as fighters in the sky
dropped hundreds of bombs on enemy artillery
positions. At daybreak orders were given for the
general advance. Thousands of infantry troops
swept across the enemy trenches. By eight o'clock
they had penetrated the enemy lines some distance
and were now in the reserve positions of the
enemy.

We started out about seven o'clock to
follow the advance. Already the results were
beginning to show. A steady stream of ambulances
was coming down the roads with the wounded, big
trucks with the wounded lying on straw went

thundering by, large batches of German prisoners
were coming down across the fields. Tanks were
bouncing over the rough terrain. Artillery came
out of hiding as horses and men tugged at the
ropes, pulling and pushing the cumbersome
carriages across the shell holes to new advance
positions. We passed mechanized trucks slowly
moving forward, holding the guide wires and cables
of observation balloons above. The observers, with
powerful glasses, were watching the advance and
reporting to the artillery, where stubborn
resistance was being encountered. We now began to
encounter considerable trouble in traveling.
Engineers were throwing dirt into the shell holes
along the road. Everything conceivable was on the
road -- gun carriages, ammunition trucks, officers
in side cars, couriers on motorcycles, field
kitchens, supply trucks going forward and
ambulances and trucks loaded with wounded bucking
traffic on the way south to the hospitals. We
passed through the villages of Mandres and
Seicheprey, the most advanced position of our
previous visits, across No Man's Land and into the
country held by the Germans for four years.
Scattered in the fields were the still forms of
American and German soldiers who had made the
supreme sacrifice.

The Germans were taken by surprise with the
swiftness and terrific drive let loose upon them.
The advance continued uninterruptedly, and by
nightfall the advance had penetrated deep into the
enemy lines. Thousands of German soldiers were
taken prisoner. It was the beginning of the end
for Germany. She could not pull reserves to defend
this sector, because the Argonne, directly to the
west of us, was threatened, and west of the
Argonne the French and English were pounding the
lines in the direction of Belgium and the German
border. For the first time I could see visions of
returning home some day.

The enemy was still offering stubborn
resistance, but there was a feeling in the air

that all was not well with Germany. The French
people seemed more gay, animated conversation
could be heard over the marble tables in the cafes
as they came out in greater numbers to talk about
the events taking place. It was a serious France
in the late spring and early summer, when the
gigantic offensive of the Germans looked as if it
might reach Paris, but now the mighty force of the
Americans was beginning to bear fruit.

We followed the advance deep into the lines
that day, reaching to Thiaucourt. We returned to
Sebastopol late the following night. We had had
little or no sleep for forty-eight hours or more,
and were tired, hungry, and covered with dirt and
bloodstains from the filthy mess they call war. In
the first two days we captured more than 16,000
prisoners, and over 400 guns, together with a vast
accumulation of material. Our casualties numbered
about 7,000.

The following morning the hospital grounds
looked like a battlefield. Wounded were lying all
around, some on stretchers, others on straw spread
on the ground. All the floor space in the various
buildings was crowded. The less seriously wounded
walked or hobbled around, bandaged in various
places. The operating rooms were working to full
capacity, doctors and nurses were visiting the
wounded, giving them shots to ease the pain until
the operating surgeons could work on them.

I walked through the grounds talking to
some of the boys, offering them cigarettes and
cheering them up the best I could. The Y.M.C.A.
personal stationed at the hut on the Hospital
grounds did great work distributing hot chocolate,
bars of chocolate and cigarettes to the wounded.
On my travels I noticed a soldier with a bandage
around his head. He seemed much older than we
youngsters. He was sitting on a box with his legs
crossed. I walked over and offered him a
cigarette. "I smoke a pipe," he said, "but maybe
my boy here'll take one." Besides him on a
stretcher was a boy about twenty-one or two; one

leg of his breeches was cut away and his leg was
bandaged from the knee up. I handed him a
cigarette. He smiled, and pointing his finger to
the man sitting on the box, he said proudly,
"That's my Dad."

For a minute I didn't say a word. "Yes,
that's right," answered the elderly man. "We
entered the army together and we've never been
separated. When the zero hour arrived we went over
the top together, and we'll be together when those
surgeons get working on you, won't we, son?"
Fortunately their wounds were not serious, and I
know they went home together, because during their
convalescent period the Armistice was declared. It
was a touching sight to see father and son
together -- the only case I know of, though there
may have been others.

For the next two or three weeks we were
going day and night, checking the location of
graves and recording the casualties.

The St. Mihiel advance eased considerably
to reduce the bulge along the line at Verdun and
the Argonne. Many of the troops from our sector
were now moving westward to go into the lines with
the First Army, preparing to drive through the
dense forest of the Argonne.

All Quiet on the Toul Front

The days and nights were quiet now. The
constant rumbling to the north, that put us to
sleep every night since March, had passed away.
The roads seemed strangely lonesome. The
surrounding villages, that a few weeks previous
had been teeming with men in Khaki, were almost
deserted.

A lone plane now and then cut across the
sky like a bird lost from the flock. The hospital
grounds had the appearance of a country estate.
Ambulances and trucks winding along the roads,
carrying their cargo of wounded, were very few.
The great drive of St. Mihiel had passed into
history and only the mopping-up remained. Four
long years of sorrow and bloodshed were coming to
an end. Peace had already arrived along the
eastern sector and was fast making its way
westward to the sea.

Amid the peaceful surroundings of the
hospital cemetery one afternoon, I had occasion to
talk with a German prisoner who was with a grave-
digging squad. I judge he was in his late forties.
I beckoned to him to come over to where I was
sitting on the bank, but he looked at the guard
who was marching up and down with fixed bayonet,
and shook his head. I asked the guard if he would
allow the prisoner to talk to me a few minutes. He
agreed, but no longer than five minutes. I was to
offer him nothing and to stay five feet away from
him. The soldier was an excellent guard. He was
right on the job and listened to our entire
conversation. Fortunately the German spoke fairly

good broken English. I was anxious to get his
reaction to all this mess.

He told me he was married and had four
children. By trade he was a baker, and owned a
little shop in one of the smaller towns outside of
Berlin. His oldest son, Carl, twenty, worked at
the ovens with him. Helen, a girl of eighteen,
helped her mother in the store, and two younger
children attended school. "We had a nice little
shop and we were very comfortable and happy. And
then 1914. Ach, why did it ever come?" and he dug
his shovel into the earth. "My son Carl left our
little home in September and we never saw him
again. Just before Christmas we got word he was
dead, and it almost broke his mother's heart. Carl
was a good boy." Tears streamed down his cheeks.
"And I loved him too. A year ago they called on
me. My wife went to the oven. She is very frail
now, but she keeps the family together." He was
glad the worst for him was over. "Some day now,"
and he looked in the direction of the German
border, "I will be back with my little family." He
asked me how many American soldiers were in
France. When I told him close to two million, he
seemed to doubt me. The German soldiers were told
that America was supplying money only, and that
the U-boats had destroyed so many ships in the
spring America had stopped sending troops across.

The very structure of war, Sashie, is built
upon lies, intrigue, vicious propaganda, and
synthetic hate. I say that because I know there is
no real hate in the hearts of the common people
who make up the nations of the earth. As we sat
and chatted along the bank of this road in France,
there never existed a born hatred between me, who
represented the conqueror, and this man, a
prisoner of the vanquished. How utterly senseless
that three weeks before the soldier with fixed
bayonet who stood beside us now, listening to this
simple exchange of thoughts, would by the ethics
of war be compelled to drive the point of that
cold steel blade into the heart of this man and

vic-versa. A Daddy who brought four good children
into this world and who loved them the same as I
do you. There is nothing new in what I am saying
to you. Daddies, hundreds of years ago, had the
same feeling, and perhaps gave vent to their
feelings the same as I am now doing to you. It
will not come in my lifetime, you may not see it
in your lifetime nor the children you bear, but
somewhere in the coming generations there will be
a time when the people of this universe will be
masters of their own souls, when they will no
longer allow demons of hell, traveling in the
robes of saintly deliverers, to lead them on to
slaughter. I saw the horrors of war, ghastly
columns of earth and steel shooting to the
heavens, mud-covered men squirming with pain on
blood-soaked fields, others with eyes wide open,
staring to the sky, but whose vision was as black
as Erebus, and yet when the notes of the bugles
carried across the fields of battle on that
November day in 1918, ending the bloody conflict,
men who moments before were trained for the kill
ran with open arms and embraced. The boundary of
hate had quickly vanished. Men were free to mingle
again. Was it because a bugle had sounded? No, it
was deep-rooted in the hearts and souls of these
men and had been for four long years.

The guard looked at his watch. The prisoner
returned to cover the burlap covering of a fallen
soldier, as I sat there, gazing at him and smoking
a cigarette. Such is the mystery of war as it was
then in 1918 and as it is now in 1940.

To the Argonne

Late in October we received word to report
for service with the First Army of the Argonne.
Barrack bags were packed and we said goodbye to
Sebastopol and the St. Mihiel Front, which had
been our home since early March. We proceeded to
Ligny-en-Barrios, First Army Headquarters. Ligny
was a quiet town, somewhat smaller than Toul, and
more suburban in looks. Big trees bordered many of
the streets. We were billeted in the center of
town at the home of an old French couple. Our
office was on the second floor, and we had two
rooms on the first floor. Canvas cots were
furnished for us.

At first it was very difficult to accustom
ourselves to this sudden change. Being cooped up
in small rooms after the outdoor life of tents. We
seemed miles away from war here. The town was
quiet and peaceful. It had been bombed by raiders
a few times, but outside of that there wasn't a
scar to be seen.

We understood this was to be our home for a
week or so, and we were then scheduled to go into
the field with the troops. McCormick, who was a
captain now, had a big military map put on the
wall. Pins marked the progress of the troops, and
we were receiving reports where the heavy
casualties were occurring, in order to locate
where our traveling would be cut to a minimum.

Captain Muckleston was now in this area,
and I saw him quite frequently.

About the first of November, an order came
through from General Headquarters of the G.R.S.
instructing me to report to the medical doctor for
a physical examination. I was to receive a
commission as Second Lieutenant. This struck me

like thunderbolt. Somehow or other I never seemed
to worry much about promotion. I enlisted as a
buck private and as far as I was concerned a
commission was far from my mind. Lack of ambition
the world would say, I guess. At any rate, I was
in line to become a shave-tail.

I was examined by a captain in the medical
corps. All the time he was fussing with me, the
smoke from his big black cigar almost chocked me.
When he got through examining me, he asked me how
many cigars I smoked in a day. I told him about
six or seven, and a half pack of cigarettes.
"Well, that's too much," he said, "you want to cut
it down to half that." Smiling, I asked, "How many
cigars do you smoke in a day, Captain?" "None of
your business," he answered, much annoyed. "I'm
the one doing the examining and asking questions
around here."

Well, that was that. I asked no more
questions, adjusted my clothing, gave him a snappy
salute to satisfy his ego, and was off.

Three or four days after we arrived in
Ligny, I was ordered to make a quick survey of
conditions along the line of advance. I traveled
in a side car. I can not recall now who was
driving. We were away three days. The weather was
miserable, raining most of the time. Going north
above Varennes on the road to Grand Pre we got
into a traffic jam worse than any we ever
encountered on the St. Mihiel front. Many of the
trucks had skidded on the slippery road, and were
settled hub high in the ditches at the sides;
other trucks with chains, trying to pull them out,
would skid, and over they would go into the ditch.

We were covered with mud. Everything you
looked at was a sea of mud. After waiting about
half an hour, we decided to try the field. We
picked up a couple of wooden planks and placed
them across the ditch, and pushed the car into the
field. We skidded and bounced over that humby
field for about a mile before we spotted a
suitable opening across the ditch to get onto the

road again. As bad as the road was, it felt like
heaven to be on it once more.

The ravages of the advance could be seen on
all sides; earth dented with shell holes,
abandoned artillery, dead horses and mules, and
miles of communication wires of the signal corps
strewn on the ground. We were some miles behind
the general advance, but the familiar sound of
artillery fire was very clear. I was carrying a
communication to be delivered to an officer in a
certain village, but in the confusion and general
mix-up I never did locate him.

The town of Ligny looked pretty good when
we rolled in, early in the morning. Filthy, tired
and hungry, even the engine seemed glad it was
over. The last forty miles coming into town we had
a lot of trouble to keep going. The constant rain
and thick coating of mud played havoc with the
engine.

The Armistice

We now heard rumors that negotiations for an armistice were going on. The Germans had requested President Wilson to outline a plan for cessation of hostilities. The President laid down his famous 14-point program as a basis for a peace among all the warring nations. This was finally agreed upon. The German delegation met Marshal Foch, Generalissimo of the Allied Armies, in a railway car in the woods at Compiegne, and signed the conditions of surrender. On November 11, 1918, at eleven o'clock in the morning, the clear notes of "cease firing" carried across the entire front. The thundering bark of cannons that France had lived with for four long years was silenced.

At eleven o'clock on that Armistice morning, we were sitting around in the office. There was no outward display of enthusiasm. We had become accustomed by this time to take everything as a matter of course. The one big thing in everyone's mind was, When do we go home? We carried two service stripes on our sleeves now. It seemed like a long time since our landing in St. Nazaire, over twelve months before. We didn't realize that a big job still lay ahead of us, and that eight more months would pass, taking us to many villages and towns in France, before our ship would steam beyond the Statue of Liberty and on to Hoboken.

About eleven thirty, Jerry Mulhern appeared in the doorway. We could see by the look in Jerry's eyes that he had been celebrating the grand event. A bottle was under each arm. He stood there for a moment, and announced in a loud voice, "The war is over! Let's have a good time!" With that, he raised one arm in salute. Down went a

bottle crashing to the floor. Someone rushed to
him and grabbed the other bottle before he decided
to salute with both arms. It was champagne. At
Jerry's suggestion, we opened the bottle and had a
drink on President Wilson.

Captain McCormick declared a holiday, so we
sent out for more champagne, and by two o'clock
the spirit of peace and happiness was well imbued.
Jerry became master of the day. He insisted that
nothing but champagne should touch our lips on
that historic day. During the day, things were
very quiet on the streets. It seemed as if the
French people needed time to adjust themselves to
the order of the times.

Darkness fell upon the town. The quietness
and solemnity of the day turned to the gayety of a
New Orleans pageant. Window shutters were opened,
the big wooden covers that hid the light of show
windows of cafes and business shops were cast
aside. Street lights that had been dead for so
long past were now throwing their glowing rays
upon the cobblestone paving.

The whole populace was on parade; horns
were blowing, regimental bands from the French and
American forces were on the march, playing the
national anthems and the airs of the popular war
songs. Mothers pushing baby carriages decorated
with the Allied Colors were in the line. Old men
struggled along, leaning heavily on a bent knotted
twig. The peasant farmers with the whole family
sitting on straw in the two-wheeled carts, with
the lantern swinging back and forth under the
axle, rattled over the rough cobblestones.

It was truly an inspiring sight. The cafes
were crowded. Player pianos and accordions were
competing for hours. Laughter and song filled the
air. We made the rounds and visited all the cafes
in town, drinking nothing but champagne. The
rising sun of the next morn still found Ligny in
the gay atmosphere of celebration.

The 12th and 13th of November didn't mean
much to our gang. Most of the time was spent on

our cots, glancing mournfully at each other and
asking the familiar question, "How in the hell do
you feel?"

Well, the war was over, and the celebration
was over.

Clermont-en-Argonne

Two or three days later we received word
that we were to proceed to Clermont-en-Argonne, to
start a recheck and locate all the graves in the
Argonne area. We realized at once that this was
some job. The Argonne drive covered many miles and
thousands of soldiers had been killed in the
terrific onslaught.

Clermont was a cold, dilapidated village,
high up in the hills, away from anywhere. It lay
about 15 miles west of Verdun, and the Aire River
wove through the foothills of the village. While
stationed here I visited Reims. The town was well
battered and the great Cathedral bore many scars
of battle. Part of the roof was completely gone,
great pieces of sculpture were entirely destroyed,
and others had great chunks of stone blown away by
exploding shrapnel.

I also visited Epernay, where I saw
thousands of bottles of sparkling champagne on the
racks in the immense vaults. Another town I
enjoyed visiting while in this vicinity was Bar-
le-Duc. It was a busy little town, and the shop
windows on the wide avenue always held my
attention. They seemed well stocked and everything
looked so attractive. The cafes were furnished
with relics of years long past. Old paintings and
engravings yellow with age hung on the walls, but
everything was neat and clean, and they served the
most excellent meals.

We were billeted in an old ramshackle
building, torn by shell-fire. Some of our troops
who had fought in the Argonne were billeted in the
village. The only redeeming feature of Clermont
was the little Salvation Army Hut where the good

women passed out honest-to-goodness doughnuts and
hot chocolate.

We were on our own once more, and had to
establish our own kitchen. A majority of the boys
of our original unity joined us again, together
with additional men of the service. We received
more transportation, and started our big job of
checking and locating some 15,000 graves. Other
G.R.S. Units were also working in this area.

Even buried in this forsaken village, life
had its amusing points. Our cook was down with a
heavy cold one day. Late in the afternoon we began
to get worried about the eats. Captain McCormick
asked if anyone in the outfit could cook a meal.
One young chap spoke up and said he was a good
cook, he hailed from the western plains, and had
cooked many a meal for the cowboys on the big
ranch located somewhere in Kansas. That sounded
pretty good to McCormick, so he was assigned to
the kitchen to prepare the meal. He was one of the
new replacements in the outfit, and no one knew
much about him -- a likeable youngster, though,
big and husky and about twenty-two years old. For
supper he gave us meatballs with dark gravy,
mashed potatoes, stewed tomatoes and coffee with
the old reliable stewed prunes for dessert.

We had been out in the open all day,
tramping over fields, and the cold, crisp air of
winter gave us a terrific appetite. The meal
looked very appetizing, but I noted a peculiar
taste, especially with the gravy. Nevertheless, I
was good and hungry, and went back for seconds.
Many of the other boys went at it again, and the
cowboy cook beamed with satisfaction.

About eight o'clock, things began to
happen. Some of the boys became sick at the
stomach. They were too sick to move off their
bunks, so we scoured around looking for buckets,
tins, boxes and any old thing that would hold the
jet black remains coming up.

McCormick, who wasn't feeling so good
himself, became alarmed, and called the cowboy.

"Say, what in the hell did you put in that grub?"
The poor boy was well scared. "Nothing, Sir, that
I know of," he answered meekly. The ones on their
feet went to the kitchen. We smelled the side of
beef hanging outside the door, we opened a can of
tomatoes, looked at the potatoes, and examined the
coffee and prunes. Everything seemed to pass
inspection. McCormick scratched his head. "Did you
fry the meat cakes with a piece of fat off the
beef?" he asked.

        "No sir, they began to stick to the pan, so
I used some of that stuff," pointing to a can on
the shelf at the side of the range.

        Buddy Eagle, the mechanic, spoke up, "Why,
you big nut, that's axle grease."

        I hit for the open and everything came up.
I had plenty of company. All we needed was a
little encouragement, and believe me, we got it.
Every time I thought of the rich, dark brown gravy
spread on the meat cakes my stomach went into
reverse.

        That was the first and last meal our
willing candidate from the western plains
officiated at, and McCormick, in no uncertain
terms, ordered Eagle to get that - - - - - - - -
can of axle grease the hell out of the kitchen.

Metz and Verdun

Captain Muckleston was now G.R.S. Officer of the First Army Area, and spend considerable time with us in Clermont. In the latter part of November we took a week-end trip to Metz. I sent Nana and Grandad the following letter, telling them all about it.

Clermont-en-Argonne,
France, Dec. 2, 1918
Dear Parents:
I am so sorry to hear of the great Flu epidemic in America. So far we, in the interior of France, have escaped the ravages of this terrible outbreak, but I understand the situation at the base ports is very serious. It seems the world is just loaded with trouble. The boys are receiving sad news in every letter coming over from home. Only tonight Jerry Mulhern received word that his brother had died and several of the other boys had received similar news.
I am glad to know, however, that it seems to be losing its force. I pray that all of you will escape this latest horror of destruction.
I want to tell you about a little trip I just finished. Captain Muckleston, who is G.R.S. officer 1st Army, and I left this village Saturday on a little pleasure jaunt. Our first stop was in Ligny-en-Barrios, the First Army headquarters. You will remember we were billeted there when the Armistic was declared.
We had dinner at the Officers' Club, and proceeded on to Neufchateau, stopping

*for a few minutes at Bar-Le-Duc to enjoy the
hospitality of this lovely town, and to warm our
inners with a couple of hennessy's. We left
Neufchateau around 5:30 and passed through Toul,
our old stamping grounds, arriving in Nancy about
7:30, where we enjoyed a swell supper at the Cafe
Lorraine.*

An amusing incident occurred here.

*Muckleston, Reds Vernon, who was
driving us, and I sat at a table directly opposite
two American officers — First Lieutentants. They
eyed us with chilly glances, and started a heated
conversation between themselves on the slipshod
discipline of the American Army. They were at a
loss to understand why an officer would be seen in
a great public place like this with enlisted men.*

*It would never be tolerated in the
German Army, they said, and in all their travels
in France, they never saw a French officer dining
with the enlisted men. They kept this jabbering up
for some time. Finally, Muckleston got up and paid
them a visit. What he told them could hardly be
recorded. It came fast and furious, and it looked
for a time as if they American Army was to start
the war all over again.*

*Muckleston is a handsome-looking
Marine, snappy uniform and built like an ox. His
parting shot was, "If he heard another remark from
their direction he'd smash them right square in
the jaw." In fact, he was willing to right then if
they wanted to leave the room and go outside.
There didn't seem to be much desire on their part
to fight the Marines, so everything quieted down.*

*We stayed in Nancy overnight, and
left bright and early Sunday morning for Metz. We
arrived here about 11 o'clock, and immediately
went on a sight-seeing tour. The town has some
traces of the French influence, but many of the
later buildings are typical German in character.
The streets are immaculate and well policed with
snappy looking soldiers.*

*It would surprise you to see this
city. All the stores are well stocked. Big sides
of beef and choice cuts are on display in the
butcher shops.*

*The women were dressed in the height
of fashion. Men with their big fur-lined
overcoats, spats and canes. The children were
warmly clad; little blonde curls peeping from
under fur caps; the boys with fur-lined gloves to
match, and the girls carrying small muffs hanging
from their shoulders by velvet straps.*

*Everyone seems to carry an air of
confidence and the snappy swing of the walking
sticks at the side of the promenaders, as they
gaily marched along, indicates to me that the
spirit of the German people is far from shattered.
The French people we saw there seemed very solemn
by comparison.*

*Judging Germany by Metz, the things
we have been hearing about on the other side of
the line seem untrue. Their living conditions and
the general atmosphere seems far superior to that
we witness in the larger cities of France. Poor
France has paid a heavy price for victory, -- if
it is a victory. The same tired faces pass you on
the Avenues, and the heaps and heaps of stone that
once were villages will be staring at them like
ghosts from a demon age for a long time to come, I
fear.*

*Is Germany to remain a conquered
nation, I wonder?*

*Around noon time we began to get
hungry, and dropped into a hotel across from the
large square in the center of town. While waiting
for dinner to be served, we played a game of
billiards.*

*For dinner, poor starved Germany gave
us Vegetable Soup, Roast Pork, Roast Potatoes,
Peas, Carrots, Pickles, and some kind of chopped
up mess of cabbage with peppers and thick
dressing. Everything touched the spot; the only*

*complaint I had was with the bread — it was almost
black and had no taste whatever.*

> *The surroundings were fine. We ate
off a big mahogany table covered by a white linen
cloth, and spread big linen napkins over our dusty
beeches.*

> *We were the only occupants in the
room at the time, and the sup-sup-sup as we
gobbled down our soup was heard only by ourselves.*

> *After dinner the Captain bought a
small box of German Cigars -- they cost 20 cents a
piece, and strong enough to knock you down. Our
meal cost about a dollar a piece.*

> *We left Metz around 1:30 and headed
for Verdun, traveling over a desolate and shell-
torn country most of the way.*

> *All Verdun is consecrated ground to
the French. It was the scene of perhaps the
bloodiest battle of the war. Thousands upon
thousands of graves spotted around the border tell
of the terrific struggles that raged there. The
town is along the Meuse and rises to a
considerable elevation. All along the slope the
houses stand, looking something like a mass of
beehives. At the summit stands the ancient
cathedral balanced by two immense towers. In
design the cathedral differs somewhat from the
typical Gothic examples you see so frequently
in France, it resembles more the early Norman,
sturdy and massive in detail.*

> *To the north facing the Belgian and
Luxembourg border, which is perhaps 25 miles
distant, stands the quaint citadel where the
French under General Petain made the gallant stand
against the Crown Prince's Army coming down the
valley from Montfaucon.*

> *A French officer kindly consented to
guide us on our visit around the town. From the
ramparts of the citadel we could see the ruined
village of Montfaucon high on the hill surrounded
by the dense forest of the Argonne. We also had a
good view of the battle-scarred town of Verdun*

from here. From the evidence the Germans poured thousands of shells within its borders.

We also visited the famous trench in the fortification where a small band of French fought to the end, refusing to leave yet knowing full well they were doomed. When we arrived here the French officer saluted and stood at attention for a full minute. It was indeed a solemn occasion.

Everything here remains untouched. The men are buried here, helmets are lying around, rifles with rusted bayonets are scattered on the ground.

The officer told us it was the intention of the Government to keep this hallowed spot intact for all time to come, symbolizing to future generations the courage and spirit of the French troops in the dark moments of the nation's history.

We left this historic spot about the time the sun was sinking beyond the dense foliage of the Argonne. There it stood, this quiet and almost deserted city of Verdun, the city of jagged walls, like the Acropolis of ancient Athens rising among the slopes. The great battles fought here are over. Time is moving on -- it will be to the historians to pen what occurred here. What they will say can only give a mental survey; a fleeting glance of the surface. The real pages are buried beneath the soil only God and the souls of those who lie silently in the rough, amid its ruins, know the full chapter.

We arrived in Clermont just in time to enjoy a typical army meal of Beef Stew, with plenty of potatoes and the everlasting stewed prunes for dessert. Talk about no such thing as perpetual motion -- well I think stewed prunes are about the nearest approach to it.

Well, Dear Parents, we had a grand trip. Some of it very amusing, and other parts of it were very serious. So it will always be in

*life, I guess. Moments of laughter and moments of
tears.*

*This existence over here has been a
wonderful education to me. I would not sell it for
a million dollars, neither would I want to buy it
again for the same amount.*

*My mind has been broadened by the
contacts I have made. I have learned to be easily
satisfied with what life has to offer. I realize
so far, with all the misery of war and the
hardships of life that are associated with it,
that I came off mighty lucky.*

*When I see the rows and rows of
crosses rising silently from the ripples in the
earth, I sometimes think how easily I could have
been represented by one of them. In our travels
Jim and I saw a few shells drop. It was just fate
I suppose that they didn't hit too close.*

*I must close now. It is almost 1:30
in the morning. I had no idea when I sat down here
on the old wooden crate and glued my candle in the
far corner that I would string this jabbering to
so many pages.*

*I suppose you realize by this time I
am what you call a spasmodic writer. There are
times when I cannot collect my thoughts at all —
when one page is an effort, and then again at
times I feel there is so much cooped up in my
brain that I can't write fast enough to get it all
on paper. Here tonight everybody is sound asleep.
I can hear the evidence all about me. Some are
snoring. Some are whistling. Some muttering
incoherent syllables -- others tossing and
turning. I notice one fellow with his blankets
dragging on the floor. Before I turn in I will
tick him in, because it will get mighty cold in
this ramshackle building before morning.*

*The way I feel now I could write
until the sun peeps over the distant hills to call
it another day, but I must just say good-night.*

Your loving Son,
John.

- -

    During the trip I noticed Muckleston was
very restless and irritable; about three weeks
later, on the advice of the Chief Medical Officer
of the area, he was relieved of his command and
ordered home on the verge of a nervous breakdown.
He asked me to accompany him to the railway
station at Neufchateau. While waiting for the
train we strolled across the street to a cafe and
had a drink; we raised our glasses. It was the
finale to a true and warm friendship.

Fontaines

Our stay at Clermont was not long. Packing day had arrived again. A dismal cold sleety afternoon found us bound northward along the main road from Verdun to Stenay and Sedan. Two months before, this road that followed the river Meuse was alive with troops, artillery, caissons, kitchen wagons and ammunition trucks on the drive through the Argonne. That afternoon it was a lonely strip of broken stone through barren waste.

To the west of this road stretched the heart of the Argonne battlefield from Malancourt and Varennes on the South to Grand Pre on the north.

About three miles south of Dun-sur-Meuse we left the main road and slowly picked our way over a rough one-lane wagon path. It was dark and the road was slippery and treacherous. Sharp curves were numerous; the terrain was hilly and in places the ground fell fast from the side of the road into the valley.

Finally we arrived at our destination — a God-forsaken village called Fontaines. The only inhabitants were a few stray dogs running around.

This hamlet had been held by the Germans since early 1914, and was used as a prison camp. On the hill at the outskirts of the town were ten or twelve large wooden barracks and a well equipped cemetery of French soldiers. This was to be our home for the next three months. We unpacked, lit our oil lanterns and started an inspection of our new quarters. From the general appearance of things the Germans had left in a hurry. Barrack stoves were in place and a good supply of wood was neatly stored in the supply room off the kitchen. By 11 o'clock we were well established. Blankets were on the bunks, fires were blazing in the stoves. The faint glow of candlelight shone on the sleet-covered branches outside the barrack windows, and the smell of hot coffee from the kitchen whiffed through the air.

McCormick established his office and quarters in a little house at the foot of the hill adjacent to the camp.

The following day we started our gigantic job of rechecking and locating the graves in the Argonne area. Squads of eight men each were formed, and the leader of each group carried a coordinated military map of the area assigned to him.

We received additional personnel and transportation, and soon had a little village of our own. The hours of the long winter nights in the black lonely hills of Fontaines were spent in various ways. Some gathered around Doosey with his accordion, where music, song and laughter swayed the air; others stretched on their bunks beside the flickering candlelight and read a book or magazine; some went cootie hunting; others patronize the home-made bar. The office vibrated with the click of typewriters, as your Uncle Jim and the other boys typed the records of the day's work. Many nights the office lights were on until one and two o'clock in the morning, with the office force working at top speed, trying to keep up to date with the records that were coming in by the hundreds.

**Commission as Second Lieutenant
Quartermaster Section
September 16, 1919**

Christmas in the Argonne

Christmas was approaching. Dick Black, who had charge of the kitchen, began to worry about the Christmas dinner. Some of the western boys suggested a good old-fashioned barbecue. Everybody fell in line with this swell idea, so we all chipped in, and Dick went over to a little village in Belgium, just over the border, and put in his order for a pig. The farmer delivered it on Christmas Eve. It looked great hanging on the hook outside the kitchen door, sliced down the center with little bunches of green tucked around it.

The fires were started Christmas morning amid great pomp and ceremony; the barbecue and the bar were the important points of interest all day. Stumpy, who measured about four feet eight inches -- the smallest soldier in the army, I believe -- was made bartender. He was in his underwear, had on a German soldier's coat with gas mask dangling in front, a German dress helmet cocked on his head, a Kaiser Wilhelm mustache worked over his lip by a black cork artist; a pair of aviator goggles, German boots that reached above his knees, and a polka dot apron tied in the middle with a bright red sash. I don't think I ever saw a comedian on the stage in a get-up quite so funny.

We soon found that Stumpy was the wrong man for the job. For every drink he passed out he had one on the house. His eyes began to get bleary and his nose began to run. His finger would go up to stop the flow and soon his mustache had spread all over his face. He was finally laid to rest about two o'clock in the afternoon -- goggles, boots and all. We folded his hands across his breast and gently laid the helmet at his head -- a fitting tribute to a gallant bartender.

About four o'clock we sat down to dinner,
and what a meal! I will never forget it. The
evening was well long before we finished. After
the meal we sang our old army ditties and ended
with Christmas hymns.

And so ended a glorious Christmas day deep
in the woods of a lonely and desolate country in
the Argonne.

Dick Black looked after the welfare of the
boys in great shape. The food was good and we were
getting a pleasing variety of meals. About once a
week we had sausages and hot cakes for breakfast,
usually on Sunday morning. A big turnout was
assured at this meal. On one of these special
mornings, some soldier with a gruesome sense of
humor put the skull, or I might say, the head of a
German soldier on the roof of the lean-to right
over the door leading to the mess hall. Patches of
skin still covered the face, and to make it more
realistic he had the hair parted in the middle. We
never found out who the bright boy was who did
this, but McCormick let it be known that any
further display of this sort of humor would
forfeit our sausage and hot-cake breakfasts. The
head was buried in the camp cemetery and a cross
erected, marking the grave of an unknown German
soldier.

In January I received a commission as
Sergeant Senior Grade, the highest non-commission
grade in our service. My commission as Lieutenant
was held up by the signing of the Armistice.
Finally an order came through stating that all
commissions not clearing before November 11th were
to be cancelled, but that unsuccessful applicants
would receive a commission as reserve officer in
the army after the war ended. I was glad it turned
out that way because it meant I was in no danger
of being transferred. I could remain with the old
gang until the end.

Toward the end of February the weather
began to break. The sun was getting high and
little patches of green began to show along the

hillsides. It had been a bleak, cold winter, with occasional heavy snows. We had not seen anyone outside of our own little party. Thousands of crosses and ruined deserted villages that made up the Argonne had been our only diversion.

A Trip to Belgium

A late Saturday in February broke clear and mild -- just like Spring. McCormick told me it was about time to step out. "How about a week-end trip into Belgium? I understand there's a lively little town called Arlon about sixty or seventy miles from the border." It was perfectly O.K. with me, so five of us jumped into our truck around noon time, bound for Belgium. It was a great trip. I was full of pep when I returned Sunday night and sat down at my soap-box desk in the quiet of my little cabin on the hilltop, and wrote Nanna this letter.

Fontaines, In the Argonne
February 23, 1919.

Dear Parents:
Well, here comes another story. It is not quite so hard to write when you have something to say. When a fellow is buried for a couple of months deep in the woods of the Argonne, seeing nothing but shell holes, wrecked artillery caissons, dead horses and mules, heaps of stone that once were villages, and crosses of the dead that meet you everywhere you turn, it does one mighty good to get away from it all for a few days.

We have been working hard here for the last two months, re-checking something like fifteen thousand graves. They are mostly scattered and cover miles of territory, all the way from Varennes to Grandpre and beyond on the north and along the Meuse on the east to the depths of the Argonne forest on the west.

As you know from the reports back home, this is where the great battle of the Argonne was fought. Parts of it is wild country, especially through the thick of the forest. We had to check every foot of this ground through the forest to make sure that all Americans were accounted for. We found only three boys who were not buried. Two we found in the thick underbrush. We noticed two helmets shattered with machine gun holes, and an open pack of mud-covered cigarettes. We stopped to pick them up and while examining them one of our fellows saw the shoes of one boy protruding from the dense thicket. Here we found two bodies side by side, one of them had the remains of a cigarette tightly clasped between his fingers. The other boy we fond under the body of a horse in a deep shell hole. Just beyond was the wrecked and shattered remains of a field artillery gun, and another horse.

Well, to get on with my story, we left this deserted little village about noon on Saturday. There were five of us -- Captain McCormick, two Lieutenants, Jerry Mulhern and I. Jerry was the driver, and we traveled in our little Ford truck. It had been a staunch old friend, but it is beginning to tire easily now. The least grade will make it spit and sputter, and we hold our breath until it reaches the level.

I have had a five minute intermission. I just captured a cootie, he must have been traveling about sixty miles an hour. The bell for the start happened when he was at my knee. I caught him going around the top of my shoulder. Upon examination I found he was of the 1919 variety, 118 wheel base and from the number of crawlers he possessed, about a 500 H.P. motor with a reverse and forward action both working at the same time. The body was painted a dark brown, sort of camouflage, you know. He usually prefers the seams in your underwear for the race track, and as he carries no headlights, can cover considerable ground before you get within hailing

distance. He had one bad feature, and that is his
break system — it has a tendency to stop quick and
dig in. Then comes your chance, you scout around
and usually find him with the hood buried deep and
the machinery in full motion. Finally, you take it
to the workshop, put it on the bench, call three
or four of your brother mechanics to look over the
movements. After close consultation the experts
agree it is a European cootie flyer, as it offers
so many disadvantages to the sporting public it is
promptly condemned to death.

I am all set again. It's funny how
little things do upset the works. Now if you take
out your map you can follow our trip. We started
just north of Verdun, trailing along the Meuse
river, passed Damvillers and Dun-sur-Meuse, then
we turned right and hit the Theinte river,
following this north to Montmedy. From here we
crossed the border into Belgium. The difference in
the architecture was quiet apparent. The main
body of the houses are usually cream color
plaster, the shutters a dark, rich brown with
bright yellow stripes around the window frames,
and the curtains are all colors of the rainbow
with neat little designs of various patterns. The
tie-backs are vivid reds and blues. The cornices
are in gay colors and the roofs are of heavy
dark slate, so different from the tile roofs of
France. Winding paths bordered with shrubbery lead
to the deep recessed entrance doorways usually
painted a deep blue. Altogether there is a
distinct flavor of quaintness about these little
homes.

We continued on over fine roads and
wonderful natural landscape, and arrived in the
town of Vitron about two o'clock. We had a lay-
over here for fifteen minutes, and enjoyed our
stroll through the quiet streets of this beautiful
town. Jerry spotted a bakery shop; one look in the
window was enough to start your teeth floating.
All sorts of pies, cakes and buns were on display,
and the aroma coming from the ovens in the back

*was just too much to resist, so we stormed the
place and stocked up with almost every item they
had. Coming out, we looked like you, Mother, on a
Saturday morning shopping tour loaded down with
paper bags galore.*

    *From here we kept on the main road
and passed through St. Ledger; at five o'clock we
reached our objective, Arlon. This is a quaint
little town about the size of Frankford. We
traveled around the town looking for a hotel, with
all the kids in the place running after us.
American soldiers are few over there, so we were
more or less of a curiosity. After a ten minute
search we arrived at the Hotel Du-Nord, a neat
little building in the center of town. We made
arrangements for our stay, and I had a very nice
room facing the rear garden. We made ourselves
presentable with a little water and a 65¢ cake of
soap, and as dinner was not served until seven
o'clock we strolled around the town window-
shopping.*

    *Passing one cafe we heard music, so
decided to stop in and pass away a few moments.
Here was a little room all dressed up in wonderful
colors. The bar made wore a checkered waist of red
and white, and a black velvet skirt with high
buttoned shoes of vivid red. She greeted us with a
big open smile that made us feel right at home.
On all sides of the room men and women were seated
on rough wooden benches, with deep veined marble-
top tables before them, sipping and chatting
peacefully. In a far-off corner sat an old man
smoking a clay pipe, a bright polka-dot
handkerchief tucked around his neck, and he was
playing an accordion.*

    *Pretty soon the place took on a
holiday atmosphere. They wanted to celebrate in
honor of their American guests. The quiet chatter
of a few minutes ago turned into laughter. The old
man's eyes sparkled and the dreamy notes from the
accordion took the quick tempo of dance music.
Couples one by one rose from the benches and were*

in the center of the floor dancing the typical
spin that we see so often in France.

    We enjoyed it immensely, and showed
our appreciation by loud applause. This pleased
the old man. He never did stop playing. The piece
that nearly took me off my feet was "When the ball
was over." Do you remember, Mother, how you would
sing we kids to sleep with that old melody. I gave
him two francs and requested that he play it
again. It was well worth the price. I don't think
I ever heard anything quite so beautiful.

    Time passed swiftly, and we arrived
at the hotel just in time for dinner, which
happened to be quite good. For dessert, we
punished a large pie that we had bought at the
shop in Vitron.

    After dinner we went to the theatre,
and what a time. We sat there for three hours
trying to figure out what it was all about. Our
party had a separate box on the second floor, and
that is where the show centered most of the time.
With the audience in tears we would be laughing
our heads off. One young actor from the stage
announced in good English, rather sarcastically, I
thought, "Ah, the Americans have a queer sense of
humor." I guess we have, because we sure made
fools of ourselves, applauding at times when we
should have been crying.

    It reached the climax when the hero
kissed the heroine's father. It struck us funny
that two men should kiss each other on the cheek,
especially when we have been leading a life like
ours for the past eighteen months, so it
immediately called for a general outburst of
hilarity from our box.

    The entire audience looked at us, as
well as the players, and the show stopped for a
couple of minutes while the principals pulled
themselves together.

    We were getting a little worried by
this time, and while we were holding a
consultation among ourselves, promising each other

to be better boys, a big fat fellow, dressed in a
long blue coat, with a gold braid and brass
buttons, entered our box. He carried a big brass
staff, with a curled embossed top, in his hand. He
was the law, and he indicated with loud voice and
many gestures that if we didn't behave -- out into
the cold night we would go. We promised to be good
and lasted the night out.

The show ended about 11:30. We were
getting ready to leave when we observed a lot of
confusion among the audience on the ground floor.
They were all milling around, grabbing chairs and
moving them to the side walls. We stood and
wondered why all this. Soon the center of the big
room was clear; the orchestra blazed forth, the
people formed in couples and the Grand March was
in full swing. It was the opening event of the big
dance that lasted until dawn. We found later this
was a general custom of the Belgian theatres on
Saturday evenings.

We looked on from the balcony,
enjoying the music and watching the native dances.
Around two o'clock we were tired, and decided to
call it a day.

I reached for my cap on the chair
beside me, but it was gone. I never did find it --
someone had taken it as an American Souvenir, I
suppose.

We ran to the hotel, a block away, in
a driving rain, and my rapidly developing bald
spot got soaking wet. You will be surprised when
you see me. My thick crop of hair is going fast --
a bare space is already showing in the back, but
outside of that, and ten or twelve extra pounds,
there is nothing new to report personally.

Sunday came upon us bright and clear.
I was awakened by the tolling of the bells in the
cathedral a short distance away. It was the first
time I had heard a church bell since November
11th, so you see the wilderness that has
surrounded us here in the depths of the Argonne.

I walked all over town Sunday morning trying to buy a military cap, but was unsuccessful. Finally I bought an English riding cap. I looked like an official war correspondent.

Around twelve o'clock we left Arlons and headed for home. We arrived in a little village called Fromerville at one-thirty, and had lunch, then posed for a few pictures. We passed through Stenay, France, and on down the main road from Sedan to Verdun.

About a mile away from our home port, Fontaines, we hit a steep grade, and our faithful Henry went back on us. We had to push him up the hill, but when we reached the top he wiggled back to life, and all was well. The end of a perfect trip.

We expect to leave here in a few weeks, and get in touch with civilization again. I am getting the nervous jitters. When will the order ever come sending us back home?

Your loving Son,
John.

P.S. I was surprised to hear that the Saturday Evening Post told a little about our experiences with the Yankee division at Mandres. I have a copy of General Pershing's Commendation, which you saw. I am enclosing it. I always have a copy of the Post tucked under my bunk and I enjoy reading about some of the things we see over here. But I missed this one entirely.

- -

Two weeks after our trip the job assigned to us was about finished. Since early December we had covered nearly every foot of ground that made up the battle field, and visited every village in the area, of some of which little remained -- only charred walls.

If you look at your school map of France, just north of the Verdun, and to the west, you will see some of the villages that made up the Argonne area: Malancourt, Vanquois, Varennes, Montblainville, Apremont, Cheppy, Very, Carpentry, Cuisy, Montfaucon, Nantillois, Brieulles, Exermont, Chatel-Chehery, Cornay, Sommerance, Flexville, Romagne, Cunel, St. Bantheville Jurin, Grandpre and on to the north.

Montfaucon was an interesting spot. The ruined village stood on a dominating hill rising more than five hundred feet high, which was the point of vantage from which the Crown Prince of Germany had watched the opening attack of his troops upon Verdun in 1915.

The whole hill had been fortified by the Germans with a number of concrete block houses, with rounded roofs, small slits were in the concrete walls, through which machine guns were fired. There was an elaborate system of concrete trenches and dug-outs extending in front of the hill. Thousands of troops could navigate without being seen from the air. The Germans took advantage of this natural setting for heavy fortifications. They figured that an allied attack coming north between the Meuse and the Argonne would be mowed down by machine gun fire.

We checked hundreds of graves, of the gallant 79th, who made the direct attack on Montfaucon, and the 37th, who flanked them on the left, at the bottom of the great hill that fortified the town. The capture of Montfaucon was the crowning achievement of the Argonne battle. The Germans long held the belief that they had created a Rock of Gibraltar where the movement of troops could be seen for miles from their elaborate observation towers, and where hundreds of machine guns nests high on the hill could spray the lowlands surrounding the mound.

We visited the observation tower, and saw the shell-torn country spread before us for miles in all directions. We looked through the little

slits of the machine gun stations down on the
fields dotted with little white crosses of the
boys of the 79th, who fought their way, foot by
foot, defying the mad snorting of guns spraying
them with steel from these hidden ramparts.

The drive through the Argonne started on
September 26th. A terrific barrage was laid over a
twenty-five mile front along the Malancourt,
Vauquois, Varennes line. The barrage began at 2:30
A.M. and lasted for four hours. More than 3000
guns were in line and the American batteries were
augmented by some thirty-five French artillery
regiments.

At the jump off, three Corps were in line.
The First Corps, composed of the 28th, 35th, and
77th Divisions under command of General Liggett,
held the line from La Harazee to Vauquois on the
eastern edge of the Aire Valley. The 37th, 79th,
and 91st Divisions held the center of the line,
driving in the direction of Montfaucon. Its
position extended from Vauquois to the slopes of
Hill 304. It was on the slopes of this hill and
the surrounding territory that the French and
German troops fought bitterly in the Battle of
Verdun during the early years of the war. The
fifth Corps was commanded by General Cameron, who
was succeeded later by General Summerall. The
Third Corps consisted of the 4th, 80th, and 33rd
Divisions, under General Bullard, and covered the
line from Hill 304 eastward to the Meuse.

On the morning of the attack, Pershing had
in line nine divisions totaling more than 300,000
men. He also had as many divisions in reserve
positions.

The advance was planned for a main attack
through the center, which was to pass through
Montfaucon. The Fifth Corps was to cover the west
flank along the Aire and the Third Corps was to
cover the east flank along the Meuse.

The objective set for the first day was to
reach the outskirts of the Kriemhilde Line north
of which the Germans had no defense system

comparable with the heavily fortified positions
surrounding Montfaucon, but the schedule was not
held. The Fifth Corps, consisting of the 37th,
79th, and 91st met terrific losses on the slopes
of Montfaucon.

The First Corps to the west also met stiff
resistance, and by nightfall they were some
distance from their objectives, Apremont and
Exermont.

The Third Corps, traveling along the Meuse,
was well on schedule, but had to drop back to
protect its flank.

On the night of September 26th the
objective for the first day, the Kriemhilde Line,
was still several miles away. This allowed the
Germans to pour reserve troops into the natural
line of fortifications this side of the Kriemhilde
Line and strengthen the dense Argonne salient. The
following days saw severe fighting. The 28th
National Guards from Pennsylvania (whose
casualties were 13,980, the largest number of any
National Guard Division) advanced to the vicinity
of Fleville. They and the First Division, who
replaced the 35th, were traveling along the
lowlands of the Aire where the Germans sprayed
them with a terrific cross fire from the village
of Cornay, opposite Fleville. Their losses were
heavy, and the advance was checked for some time;
but on October 8th, by the brilliant achievements
of the 28th, 77th, and 82nd, the villages of
Cornay and Chatel Chehery were captured. The
Argonne salient was gradually being mopped up, and
by November 1st Grandpre and St. Juvin strong
holds along the Kriemhilde Line were in our
possession.

From November 1st until November 11th the
advance moved forward rapidly, passing Bezancy and
on to Sedan, where troops from the 42nd Rainbow
Division were the first to enter. On November
11th, the last day of battle, the 90th Division
entered Stenay, where the German Crown Prince
lived for some time during the war.

In the Meuse-Argonne offensive the
Americans captured over 26,000 prisoners, 4000
guns, including machine guns, and our loss was
about 118,000 wounded and killed.

Before leaving this area, McCormick and I
visited the proposed shell-dented site for the
American National Cemetery in the Argonne. Some
thirty thousand crosses spread in solemn rows now
mark the resting spot of the men who died in
battle. The cemetery is situated outside the
village of Romagne in the heart of the Meuse-
Argonne battlefield.

In early March we left the desolate wastes
of the Argonne and headed south for Souilly, a
town lying southwest of Verdun.

Souilly was a great railroad center. During
the battle and the long siege of Verdun, the
French used the spot as a center of communication
and supply base. It was here that General Petain,
the defender of Verdun, made his headquarters
during the early days of the war. A large hospital
consisting of many wooden barracks lined the
sloping hills beyond the great railroad yards. Our
stay here was short, our work consisting of
checking records in French cemeteries and one
fairly large American plot just south of Verdun.

From here we went to Layecourt, a base
hospital center, where we occupied an abandoned
hospital suite of wooden barracks, and for the
first time in my army career I had a private room.
We had a swell layout here and enjoyed ourselves
for a couple of weeks. The kitchen was fully
equipped with a big modern stove and a delightful
mess hall to dine in.

St. Patrick's Day was drawing close, and we
decided to have a party, in fact two parties.
Captain McCormick was giving a party in the big
mess hall. He invited the officers and nurses from
the hospital, together with a few of the leading
French citizens. We were busy decorating the hall
two days in advance. French and American colors
were draped from the ceiling, and captured

trophies from the battlefields adorned the side
walls, the long tables were covered with green
bunting, clay pipes with green ribbon bows were at
each plate, as well as colorful head-pieces of
every description.

Doosey had been engaged to furnish the
music, and Bill Lenox was to lend his mellow voice
to grace the occasion. The guests arrived, and it
was truly a colorful set-out.

We were standing on boxes and chairs
looking in the high windows. Doosey and Lenox were
seated at the head of the tables. Bill Doosey was
already imbued with the spirit of St. Patrick,
having celebrated at the opening round of our
little party.

In front of McCormick was a small silver
cup, something like a prize trophy handed out at a
race meet. He stood up, holding the vessel.
"Before we start festivities," he said, "let us
all sip from the loving cup in honor of St.
Patrick. I will start it off with our honored
accordionist." He passed it to Doosey, who had
been busily engaged talking to Lenox when
McCormick announced the procedure. When Bill saw
the cup his mouth took on a grin from ear to ear.
He took a couple of good healthy embraces, smacked
his lips, rolled his eyes, and then for the kill.
The loving cup went high in the air as Bill
drained the contents.

The host was embarrassed, the crowd went
wild, and Doosey went south. He started to play,
it carried for a while, but soon it died away.

Shortly after we started our own
celebration, and I will never forget St. Patrick's
night of '19 in Layecourt, France -- nor, might I
add, the morning after.

Goncourt Again

April found us back in the little village
of Goncourt, where we had spent the winter of 1917
and 1918. It felt like old times to be here again,
along the peaceful valley of the Meuse and the
home of Yvonne.

The little oak-lined room was just the
same. She was sitting on a bench on the rough
stone terrace in front of the cafe, knitting, as
we trudged up the hill. She wore a black dress
trimmed with dainty lace at the collar and
sleeves. Her golden hair was parted in the middle,
and her plaits tied with little ribbon bows fell
upon her shoulders.

I had traveled far since I last saw her,
but I never met anyone quite like her since my
departure. We sat on the bench and talked for a
long time. Her mother called her to supper, and
she invited me to eat with her, but I excused
myself and ambled on down the hill to the
barracks.

After mess I returned, and we sat in our
favorite corner in that quaint little room. While
the gang made merry I told her about our travels
and experiences. "Now you know France. You have
seen it as I know it here in the stillness and the
beauty of the valley. Where the waters of the
Meuse roll peacefully on to the headwaters of the
north, and you have seen it as fathers and sons,
the men of France, have for four long years. Tell
me, " she asked excitedly, "is it terrible like
the pictures show? Are the forests just dead
sticks of wood, and is it true that villages are
piles of stone?"

"Yes," I answered, "it is like the pictures
show, the ravages of war have truly left their

mark in your northern land, but the spirit of your
men who are resting amid the ruins will not let it
remain so. A new land will flourish. New and
beautiful villages will rise from the crumbled
stones of the old. Young saplings will mingle with
the dead wood, and soon hide the battle-scarred
veterans of the forests. Farmers will plow the
shell-dented fields, and new crops will spring
from the earth again to bask in the sunlight, and
bring abundance to you, and grain and hay for the
cattle."

"Ah, it is a beautiful picture," she said
slowly. "I pray it is so. It will take France a
long time, I fear, to be herself. Death and
heartache have branded us deeper than we perhaps
realize now. Look upon the faces in my little
peasant village, they are not the jubilant faces
of conquerors -- no, they are the careworn masks
of four years' misery. France is tired. The towns
may appear gay, but the peasant is the heart of
France. He is dazed -- tired, tired of war. He
will not forget."

We talked long that night. I was surprised
to find her in such a serious frame of mind. Her
simple and logical approach to the problems and
conditions of her country made her seem like a
much older person.

I had expected to have a gay reunion that
evening, but it turned out to be a sombre affair;
the little mademoiselle of Goncourt was in no mood
for celebration. Victory had arrived at a terrific
price. What it would mean to the new France rising
from the misery of the old, was her concern, as I
analyzed her reasoning.

Walking along the dark road to the barracks
that night, I began to wonder what I knew about
the country. I had lived in it for many months.
True, I had traveled far, and had seen a lot, but
did a youngster of twenty-four, hardened to the
life a soldier is accustomed to living, just for
what the next day might bring, realize the inner

thoughts of the people who made up the nation of
France?

My life in France was not that of a
theorist or dreamer -- it was a hard, callous
existence, meeting conditions as they happened. I
dropped my blankets anywhere that offered a haven
of rest. I worked hard when the occasion arose,
and I played hard when the shackles loosened. War
was my business, and I built a stiff reserve to
fortify myself against the normal emotions of life
as I knew it in America.

Our work now was confined to checking
graves of American soldiers buried in French
cemeteries, located in the small villages
throughout the area occupied by American troops.

We were now some distance behind the line
of action. Soldiers who had died from natural
causes, while in training, were buried in these
villages, and this necessitated a check of all
cemeteries over a wide area. While here, we
received the following letter from our Colonel.

April 19, 1919.

G.R.S.
Bulletin No. 22

*1. The following letter is published to the
Headquarters forces, Field Units, and all attached
organizations of the Graves Registration Service,
now numbering a personnel of nearly 10,000
unwearying and earnest workers in behalf of the
sorrowing households of our homeland; and the
Chief of the Service desires to add his own hearty
congratulations that their unselfish efforts have
been observed and acknowledged in this historic
and valued letter from the Commander-in-Chief.*

*2. It reaches us on the Eve of Easter Day,
and it happily suggest a victory over all
elemental*

*difficulties in the great work that has engaged
us, and brings to us the satisfaction that always
glorifies the consciousness of having served.*

CHARLES C. PIERCE
Lieut. Col. Q.M.C., U.S.A.
Chief, G.R.S.

AMERICAN EXPEDITIONARY FORCES
OFFICE OF THE COMMANDER-IN-CHIEF

France, March 28, 1919.

Lieut. Col. Charles C. Pierce, Q.M.Corps,
Chief, Graves Registration Service,
American Expeditionary Forces.

My Dear Colonel:

It is a pleasure for me to express my
thanks and the thanks of the officers and men of
the American Expeditionary Forces to you and your
personnel, for the efficient work of the Graves
Registration Service throughout the war.

You arrived in France, a lone advance
agent of a branch of service which had still to be
organized and which war's exigencies and hazards
made imperative.You and your first handful of
workers labored unceasingly, over-came obstacles,
taxed your brains and hands to the utmost and
finally achieved an organization worthy of the
highest praise.

On every battle-field where Americans
were engaged, and, having made the supreme
sacrifice, were laid to Their final rest, the
results of your Service were seen.

*Your personnel toiled, often exposed to the
same dangers as front line troops, and performed
their duties there diligently, conscientiously and
sympathetically. The liaison they maintained with
our Allies was admirable.*

*The consecrated service you rendered to the
kinfolk of our soldiers in conveying information
and allaying undue anxiety and fears, the part you
played in acting as personal representatives for
thousands of soldier's relatives, meets not only
with the appreciation of the entire American
Expeditionary Forces, but the gratitude of the
American people.*

*A work, so comprehensive in its scope, yet
characterized by an humanitarianism that is indeed
laudable, stands forth in bold relief as a labor
of duty and sympathy that will be a credit to our
country forever.*

Sincerely yours,

(Signed) JOHN J. PERSHING.

- -

Our stay in this little village of
Goncourt, lying deep in the valley of the Meuse
where the sparkling waters flowed in graceful
curves among the wooded lowlands, was coming to a
close. My last night with Yvonne was to be like
our parting of many months ago. We sat in the
corner of that little room and talked, while
laughter and song echoed from the walls.
She seemed cheerful; before her was a small
glass of wine which she slowly sipped as she
watched Doosey, in the center of the room, swaying
from side to side as his fingers danced up and
down the keyboard of his accordion. Her mother sat
at the corner of the bar, with chubby red face
beaming in smiles, in her white apron, while Dad

passed around the tables, serving the wants of the
boys. I looked around the smoke filled room at the
smiling faces. I watched Yvonne as she sat there,
fumbling the little black cross and silver corpus
that hung form her neck, and wondered. We would be
many miles away when darkness fell again, and the
little family of Goncourt we would see no more. No
one in the room, outside of myself, knew we were
scheduled to leave the following afternoon.

I had met Captain McCormick on my way to
the cafe. He told me we were leaving for Troyes,
about 150 kilometers from Paris. He ordered me to
get all details in by two o'clock the following
afternoon, and be ready to leave by four o'clock.

The hours passed, and all good things must
end. Before we left I asked Doosey to play
"There's a Long, Long Trail." As the boys were
about to leave, I nudged Bill. "How about
'Goodnight, Ladies'?" The soft notes floated
through the smoky atmosphere. The boys stood
facing Yvonne, and with glasses raised chimed in.
A tinge of pink came to her cheeks, as she stood
there nervously fingering the bow on her plait
that hung across her shoulder. When the last note
had died away, she bowed and walked out on the
terrace. It was the gang's unknowing farewell to a
good little lady. I watched them go down the hill,
and they would not return, and shortly I, too,
would follow.

The night was quiet now; a gently breeze
swept across the terrace. The lamp at the window
threw a faint glow along the rough stone paving,
and the little diamond chips in my mother's ring
sparkled as the movements of her thin hand caught
the rays. I had a long since made up my mind about
the ring; it was to stay with her. We sat on the
bench and talked. "It has been a wonderful night,
Yvonne. Tell me, did you enjoy it?"

"Ah, if every night could be so," she said,
slowly, "filled with music, laughter and song. But
it cannot be; soon France will be alone again. The
petite villages will be serious and quiet like the

valleys, the forests and the streams. The tramp of
feet, the shout of sharp commands rolling down the
winding roads, the happy smiles that gave us
courage -- all these will pass on to the west
again. France will miss them. Yes, I will miss
them -- such a night as this will never come
again. It is good that God gave us little prison
cells where the memories we cherish can be tightly
sealed, where no one dare enter to carry them
away."

"You have not seen France as I know it,"
she continued slowly. "You have seen it as a
soldier, dressed in the grim cloth of war, but I
trust you will carry something from our land that
will make you forget the cruel life France
beckoned you to."

"I will take something home with me -- the
memory of a brave and charming Mademoiselle, who
lives in the quiet of a beautiful valley. May it
be for her always as it is tonight."

The minutes clicked away, the light in the
window grew dim. I embraced her for the first and
last time. Somewhere somebody said,

". . . Parting is such sweet
sorrow, That I shall say good-night, till it be
morrow."

She knew now it meant farewell. I hurried
down the steps. "Your ring, your ring!" she
called. I looked back — she was standing with
outstretched hands, holding it high, as I passed
off into the darkness.

I never saw her again. I reached the bottom
of the hill and stopped. Ideas were playing leap-
frog in my young brain. I sat down on the curb of
the little watering fountain in the center of the
square and listened to my thoughts, while the game
went merrily on.

Finally I arose and headed for the
barracks. To America and the greatest girl in all
the land. You can guess, Sashie, who she is.

Fate is a strange creature. A step forward or backward as you travel through this game of life can mean so much. As you go through life there will be times when the currents of emotion will send vivid sparks crashing through the tiny cells that guide your destiny. They will yell for action, but guard yourself. Find a seat at the foot of a fountain, in the quiet of yourself reason what is best, and be the master of your own thoughts.

In troubled France today, I wonder many times what part Fate has called upon her to play. It seems true what she told me many years ago in that little room, that France must have wars just to exist. Is she still living in the quiet of the valley? Is her solemn face covered with the mask of sorrow? Was Fate so cruel as to bear her a son to lose in battle?

Farewell to Goncourt

The following noon saw us making
preparations for our departure. I was alone in the
supply room. McCormick entered. "John, what about
your mother's ring?" "Well, what about it?" I
answered sharply. "Did you get it last night?"
"No, and what's more, I don't intend to get it,"
and I walked into the other room. McCormick sensed
I was in no mood for talking. "All right,
Sergeant," he said, with a wave of his arm, and
walked out.

In the late afternoon we crossed the river
Meuse and left the village. I watched it fade and
mingle with the landscape. Only little curls of
smoke appeared now blending with sky from the wood
fires. Soon the blackened pots swinging from the
rusty cranes would begin to sing. The peasants
would take their wine bottles from the cupboard
and gather around the open hearth for the evening
meal. They would be alone; the barracks along the
Meuse would be dark and lonely, and the little
room on the hill, that rocked with music and song
a short time before, would be strangely silent,
with one little person sitting there.

As darkness fell, and I sat in the back of
the truck, bouncing over the rough roads, I
wondered what she was doing.

Troyes

Troyes is a beautiful town, lying about 150 kilometers southeast of Paris. While we were here some of the boys visited Paris. I regret that I did not avail myself of the opportunity to visit this great city while we were there, but like many other things you do in this world, I put it off until it was too late. We were billeted close to the canal, quaint little bridges crossed the narrow span at intervals, and horses slowly trod along the dirt towpath lined with trees, pulling on the heavy ropes attached to the canal boats. Old men with polka dot handkerchiefs tucked around their necks, and velvet jackets, trotted along at the head of the horses.

In the center of the town was a beautiful promenade extending perhaps a mile. It was spotted with big old trees, and floral designs of every description were spread over the smooth grass lawn. It was a beautiful sight on Sunday afternoons to see the people promenading along the gravel paths in their gay colors of early Spring. The ancient Gothic Cathedral, with the highly carved stone spires rising high in the sky, was very impressive. I made a few sketches in my notebook, as I had done in Toul and Nancy, of the various little details that interested me most.

Here we witnessed for the first time the French Fire Department in action. A fire broke out in a building a short distance from our barracks. We heard the clanging of the bells, and people were running in all directions. We joined in the parade. Smoke was pouring form the third floor window, and flames were licking through the roof. I never witnessed such a spectacle before. As the apparatus arrived the firemen jumped off, and

stood at attention in groups. The Chief, wearing a
white rubber coat and helmet, stood off to one
side with a big horn decorated with red corded
rope.

Everything was done with military
precision. No one moved until given the command
from the chief. Soon the horn sounded; the firemen
rushed to the wagons and pulled the ladders to the
street; others grabbed the lines of hose and
dragged them to the water connection. During all
this it seemed like the tower of Babel, they were
all yelling at the same time.

The horn sounded again; the men rushed the
ladders against the building; the men stood at the
bottom of the ladders with hose, but no attempt
was made to ascend until the command was given.
Likewise, I suppose they would stay on the ladder
until they dropped to the ground, if the command
was not sounded to retreat.

It hit us funny to watch these queer
antics. It brought back to my mind Nero and his
fiddle. At any rate, they put the fire out, but it
struck me there was plenty of lost motion and lots
of room for improvement in the French method of
fighting fires. I am afraid if they were called on
to fight the fires of some of our frame structures
here the buildings would be razed before the
second command sounded.

As I recall, we were not burdened with many
official duties during our short stay here. The
weather was fine, and we spent quite a few
afternoons playing catch on the street fronting
the barracks. The French people seemed very
curious and stood watching us, gesticulating and
jabbering to each other. It may have truck them
just as funny to see us standing for hours
throwing a ball back and forth to each other, and
enjoying it, as it was for us to watch their fire-
eaters in action.

While here, I received a check from home.
One afternoon Tillie La Fue and I paid a visit to
the bank to see if we could cash it. We met a

matronly-looking woman, about forty-five years
old, at the counter, and I explained to her in my
Yankee French what I wanted, who I was, where I
was from, and that it was a good check, etc. I
didn't seem to be making much headway. She just
stood there with a faint smile curled around her
lips. Could it be she didn't understand? I started
all over again; this time Tillie chimed in and
fortified my French. We both worked ourselves into
a lather heat. This was serious business to me; I
needed the money. Finally, a broad smile broke
over her face. She planted both arms on the
counter, and in better English than I ever used,
said, "Well, soldier, what seems to be the
trouble? Speak up now; maybe I can help you." We
had a good round of laughs. She came from New York
State and was the English interpreter for the Bank
and handled all their English and American
connections. I received my money and we went
happily on our way.

Semur

Soon packing day was with us again, and we were ordered to proceed to Semur, about seventy-five kilometers south of Troyes. This was perhaps the most picturesque town we had visited in all of France.

A deep ravine separated the town an a beautiful stone viaduct carried the road across the depth of the valley. A great elevation arose on one side with huge stone retaining walls supporting the sharp rise of the earthen slope.

A great castle was perched on the highest peak. Weather-beaten stone battlement towers that had faced the strong winds, sleet and storms for ages, stood silently among the trees. Many artists have traveled far to visit this location, which the hand of nature has endowed so generously with the wonders of the nature. Many times I sat on the coping of the rampart walls and looked down into the great depth of the valley. I sat there many times and watched the sun set beyond the hills many miles in the distance, and in the darkness of the night I walked up the winding road and looked down upon the sparkling lights of the town below. It was truly a fairyland.

I wondered many times on these quiet excursions how small we humans really were. Just the privilege of being created, to see in a fleeting glance the workings of the Creator stretched before us, should be enough to take the egotism and self-centered dominance away from any man. And yet the mission that called me to travel miles across the sea was in defiance of all that I saw spread before me.

You must be patient, Sashie, with these little by-way sermons that seem to creep into this

little story every now and then, but the vivid
contrast of a country in so many short miles,
makes one wonder at times how horrible man can be.
Why is it we spent the winter amid the lonely
fields of Argonne, where crosses of battle dead
seemed to spurt from the ground like mushrooms
through the mist of early dawn, where the earth
rose and fell in great crater swells like the
ocean in a great storm, and where tiny villages
that meant home to thousands, were reduced to mere
heaps of stone, and then to spend the spring in a
land such as this, untouched by the ravages of
war? I don't know the answer, but there is one
thing I do know. We have a long way yet to travel,
we are still keeping very close company with the
caveman of the early ages.

The people of Semur were very hospitable.
We were the only Americans in town, and to all
intents and purposes the place was ours. While
here our Company was augmented with ten or fifteen
more boys with motorcycles and side-cars to help
us cover the numerous French village cemeteries
scattered over a wide area. Summer was approaching
and the Government was anxious for us to finish
our work as soon as possible.

We were now wearing our third service
strip, and most of the American Army outside of
the Army of Occupation stationed in Germany had
already left the shores of France. We, too, were
getting anxious to get home.

We were billeted in an old wooden barrack
on a quiet street just off the center of town.
Directly across the street from the barrack was
the old prison of Semur, a cold, gray stone wall
surrounded the bleak buildings inside. The heavy
wooden gate with small peep-holes and supported by
massive iron strap hinges, centered directly in
front of our barracks. I got well acquainted with
the old guard who sat on a chair just outside the
gate. His one and only greeting every time I saw
him was, "Tres chaud, Monsieur." It made no
difference what the weather happened to be --

sunshine, rain, warm or chilly, it was always the
same greeting. To us it means "Very hot, Sir." He
was an immense man, about six feet two inches
tall, and weighted about two hundred sixty pounds,
with a well rounded stomach. The complexion on his
face looked like the deep red of the setting sun,
and as I picture him now, I guess he was "<u>tres
chaud</u>" most of the time.

We had many a chat together. One afternoon
he invited me to walk around the prison grounds
with him. He also took me into some of the
buildings. We passed down a tier of cells; a faint
ray of light from little bored slits in the thick,
stone wall was the only connection with the
outside world, and the sour, musty smell from
years of poor ventilation was almost sickening. I
was mighty glad to get into the open and see the
sunshine once again. Coming down the road to the
gate, he told me this was the last walk of the
condemned of years ago; that the big gate swung
open and they walked across the road where death
and the guillotine awaited them. A little curious,
I asked him where the guillotine stood. He told me
opposite the gate, and at the exact spot where our
barrack was now located. I don't know whether he
was trying to have fun with me or not, but that
night I saw more guillotines than I ever wanted to
see again in my life.

While in Semur we struck upon a French
custom that was entirely new to us. Every week-end
the peasants in the villages would travel to
different villages throughout the area. Each
village had its turn in the celebration. Old
rickety farm wagons, loaded with women and
children, old people and young people on bicycles
and a few in old chuggy automobiles came for miles
and gathered in the village.

Saturday night was usually set aside for
dancing and pleasant chatter at the tables in the
main cafe of the village. Every village, no matter
how small, always had one large cafe and one or
more smaller ones.

These places are not to be confused with
cafes as we know them here in America. As a rule
the main cafe was situated close to the village
square, where the watering fountain was located,
and the focal point of all activities. It was a
large room and very simply furnished. Perhaps a
few old prints wrinkled and yellow with age hung
on the rough plastered and whitewashed walls,
simple pine benches, tables and chairs rested on
the wide oak plank floors that sagged in the
middle from years of settlement. A little bar ran
along the short wall with assorted bottles of
choicest wine and Three Star Cognac. Sometimes
you'd find an old player piano tucked in the
corner, that rolled off notes of the Gay Nineties
vintage. The rear of the main room usually opened
to a flagstone terrace where tables were placed,
so that in pleasant weather you could enjoy the
quiet and beauty of the garden yard beyond.
Sunday morning the little village church
was overflowing, and at the close of Mass the
parish priest stood on the steps of the church and
gave his blessing to the gathering. The rest of
the day was spent in various ways, some sitting in
the shade of the big trees playing a quiet game of
cards and sipping wine; others bowling on the
greens of the garden yard to the rear of the cafe,
while others sang and danced in their native way.
The children played "ring-around-a-rosy" an other
games such as our little children play here.
Coming on to night, they would assemble for a song
fest, and after that cheek-kissing would begin and
all would be over. The rickety old wagons, the
bicycles and the chugging cars would wind their
way along the silent roads to the scattered
villages whence they came.
We heard about these little shindigs
shortly after we arrived in Semur. So, like native
Frenchmen, we too traveled on week-ends. I have
many happy memories of these pleasant little
excursions spent with the peasants of France, and

joining in the little pleasures that life offered
them.

The Dance

Toward the end of our stay in Semur the folks decided to hold a gala dance in our honor. We were the only Americans in town, and likely the last they would see. The Committee was formed to arrange the details, made up, as I remember it, of five Americans and five of the town people. We hired the hall and made arrangements for the orchestra and a good supply of refreshments.

We had a grand time. The crowd started to assemble around five o'clock Saturday afternoon. At the four walls of the big hall, gaily decked in the American and French colors, chairs were arranged where the older folks sat and enjoyed the frolicking of the younger set. We opened with a Grand March, and then went into French tail-spins that nearly finished us. How the French can stand on a dance floor all through an evening and do these native spin dances is more than I can reason. Around eleven o'clock, however, we had the orchestra breaking in with good old-fashioned waltzes, and some of the old army songs which we danced to.

Well, the lights in the hall blazed all night thorugh. Music never ceased. When the orchestra rested the player piano came into action.

An armistice was declared from nine o'clock until noon Sunday, to allow the folks time to go to church. Shortly after noon the barrage opened again, and lasted until late Sunday night.

I had all the dancing I wanted for a long time to come. Nevertheless, the affair was a grand success. We all had a wonderful time and I imagined the people of Semur still talk and

reminisce about the night of the big French-
American Dance.

The next day I received somewhat of a
shock. McCormick called the committee together, of
which I was one. "The little Frenchman," he said,
"who had the refreshment concession at the dance
tells me the American Committee owes him one
hundred and twenty-three francs for refreshments,
so you better dig into your jeans and go down and
square up."

We told McCormick the understanding was
that our Committee was to wear a little bow of
red, white and blue ribbon on our coat, and the
French Committee would do likewise with their
colors, and that we were entitled to free
refreshments. "Well, that's all right," the
Captain answered with a big grin, "but it didn't
entitle you to treat the whole population. Why, I
had about five cheese sandwiches, a bottle of
pickles and four or five glasses of beer myself on
the invitation of your big hearted committee. The
Frenchman," he went on, "understands the
arrangements all right, he's just checking up on
the side bets. So you'd better get right down
there and come across."

Well, the dance cost the big-hearted
American Committee about twenty-five dollars, but
it was well worth it. At least it helped others to
have a good time.

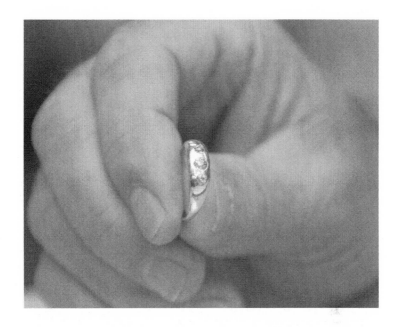

McCormick gives John his
mother's ring back. The ring can be
seen on the front cover, he always
wore it on his left pinky.

On to America

Toward the end of June our work in this area was finished. We received orders to proceed to Neufchateau, the clearing station for troops in this area going to the base ports. Our task was over. After staying at Neufchateau for three or four days, we boarded our de luxe Pullmans for Brest. This was our first experience in traveling in the famous 40 hommes, 8 chevaux (40 men, 8 horses) box cars. It was a slow, tiresome ride; sleeping on straw and bumping over the rails on flat wheeled trucks.

We arrived at the camp in Brest, where we went through the usual routine of departing -- delousing and rigid physical examination. Soon we were marching on the cobble-paved streets of France for the last time. We traveled through the city to great harbor, where many ships lay in mid-stream. We were ferried out to a large liner swinging on the heavy chains of the anchor. Billows of smoke poured from the great funnels as we boarded her, and soon the big propellers churned the quiet waters into a foaming swirl, and the great German liner, the Kaiser Wilhelm der Grosse, pointed her nose to the west and home.

Our accommodations and food were a pleasant contrast to our trip over on the old Tenedores.

One day McCormick called me to his stateroom. "I have a little surprise for you," he said, as he handed me a tiny package. I opened it. My mother's ring. "How did you get this?" I asked rather heatedly.

"A half hour before we left Goncourt, I went up to bid Yvonne goodbye, and she insisted on my taking it." Well, there wasn't much I could do

about it then. The last tie with France was
broken.

Nanna's hair changed from jet
black to silky white and she looked
much older then.

New York

We entered the great harbor of New York.
The Statue of Liberty and the skyline of New York,
with masses of stone towering high in the heavens,
appeared in the haze of early morning. Great
crowds lined the dock, waving and cheering as the
little tugs chugged and snorted, maneuvering our
giant vessel to the slip. After the ship docked,
Uncle Jim and I rushed to the big reception room,
anxiously looking for familiar faces. Pretty soon
we spotted Nanna and Grandad in the huge crowd.
Everybody was in a state of confusion, all
rushing to greet their loved ones.

It was a wonderful sight. Tears of joy
trickled down the cheeks of many, as they embraced
for the first time in many months.

Nanna had changed considerably. She looked
much older; her hair, that was jet black when we
last saw her, twenty-two months before, was now a
silky white. We could see she too was wearing
service stripes. It was great to be home. Tongues
wagged at the fast pace, as we all tried to tell
every thing that had happened in the hour allotted
to us before we started for Camp Merritt, in New
Jersey.

Time passed swiftly, and before we
realized, the sharp command came to assemble for
our departure. We all said goodbye, but not for
long. After a short stay at Merritt we were
transferred to Camp Dix, where we received hour
Honorable Discharge and sixty-dollar bonus. We
arrived home about four o'clock in the terrific
heat of a late July afternoon.

At five o'clock I was sitting in the barber
chair in Ralph's barber shop, all decked out in my
Palm Beach suit, that Nanna had to slice here and

there before I could get into it. The big
adventure was over. I was no longer a soldier,
just a happy, care-free youngster getting all
dolled up for the big welcoming-home party Nanna
was giving for us that evening.

**Nanna introduced Sara to John
summer of 1919 at Beach Haven
Terrace, New Jersey**

Finale

I spent the rest of the summer at the shore. It felt might good to see Nanna's cottage once more and to renew old acquaintances. Many hours were spent sailing on the broad waters of Little Egg Harbor. The evenings found us playing cards, dancing in the small community hall, or on the beach, where the gang would gather and sit around the flaming logs, singing and roasting marshmallows.

The curtain was falling fast along the path I had traveled in Khaki. The last note of Taps had mingled with the breeze, and the new life was starting afresh for me. Soon I was to meet the girl who was to share it with me these many years. Nanna introduced me to her late that summer. After she had left, Nanna turned to me and said, "Don't you think she's a grand girl?" I nodded in agreement, as we stood there and watched her walking toward the beach. This past summer I watched her traveling over the same path toward the beach, but this time she was not alone -- you were by her side, as I know you will always be. A wonderful mother she has been to you, and a great pal to me. We have marched together with full pack, in fair weather and stormy weather, and she is still the grand girl of twenty-one summers ago.

Well, Sashie, this is about all I have to say. The twine is unraveled, the spool is bare, and now I turn it over to you to pass along the journey of life.

Sashie's wedding day with her father, June 7, 1952, at their home in Philadelphia, PA

58483467R00114

Made in the USA
Columbia, SC
23 May 2019